How to Sell a Service

The Institute of Marketing

Marketing means Business

The Institute of Marketing was founded in 1911.
It is now the largest and most successful marketing
management organisation in Europe with over
20,000 members and 16,000 students throughout
the world. The Institute is a democratic
organisation and is run for the members by the
members with the assistance of a permanent staff
headed by the Director General. The
Headquarters of the Institute are at Moor Hall,
Cookham, near Maidenhead, in Berkshire.

Objectives: The objectives of the Institute are to
develop knowledge about marketing, to provide
services for members and registered students and
to make the principles and practices of marketing
more widely known and used throughout industry
and commerce.

Range of activities: The Institute's activities are
divided into four main areas:
    Membership and membership activities
    Corporate activities
    Marketing education
    Marketing training

OTHER TITLES IN THE SERIES

The Marketing Book
Michael J. Baker (Editor)

The Strategy of Distribution
Management
Martin Christopher

Marketing Communications
Colin J. Coulson-Thomas

The Marketing of Services
Donald Cowell

Marketing Research for Managers
Sunny Crouch

Case Studies in International
Marketing
Peter Doyle and Norman Hart

The Principles and Practice of Selling
Alan Gillam

Essentials of Statistics in Marketing
*C. S. Greensted, A. K. S. Jardine and
J. D. Macfarlane*

A Career in Marketing, Advertising
and Public Relations
N. A. Hart and G. W. Lamb

Glossary of Marketing Terms
N. A. Hart and J. Stapleton

The Practice of Advertising
N. A. Hart and J. O'Connor

The Principles and Practice of Export
Marketing
E. P. Hibbert

Sales Force Incentives
George Holmes and Neville I. Smith

The Practice of Public Relations
Wilfred Howard

Legal Aspects of Marketing
J. L. Livermore

Economics
F. Livesey

Marketing Plans: how to prepare
them; how to use them
Malcolm H. B. McDonald

Case Studies in Marketing,
Advertising and Public Relations
Colin McIver

International Marketing
S. J. Paliwoda

Business Analysis for Marketing
Managers
L. A. Rogers

Effective Sales Management
John Strafford and Colin Grant

The Marketing Digest
*Michael J. Thomas and Norman E.
Waite* (Editors)

Profitable Product Management
John Ward

Behavioural Aspects of Marketing
K. Williams

Business Organization
R. J. Williamson

The Fundamentals and Practice of
Marketing
J. Wilmshurst

Management Controls and Marketing
Planning
R. M. S. Wilson

Bargaining for Results
John Winkler

Pricing for Results
John Winkler

How to Sell a Service

Guidelines for effective selling
in a service business

Second edition

Malcolm H. B. McDonald
MA(Oxon), MSc., Ph.D, FInst.M

with

John W. Leppard
MPhil.

Published on behalf of the Institute of Marketing

Heinemann Professional Publishing

Heinemann Professional Publishing Ltd
Halley Court, Jordan Hill, Oxford OX2 8EJ

OXFORD   LONDON   MELBOURNE   AUCKLAND   SINGAPORE
IBADAN   NAIROBI   GABORONE   KINGSTON

First published 1986
Reprinted 1987 (twice)
Second edition 1988
Reprinted 1989

Written in association with John Leppard

British Library Cataloguing in Publication Data
McDonald, Malcolm, *1938–*
    How to sell a service. – 2nd ed.
    1. Service industries. Salesmanship – Manuals
    I. Title   II. Leppard, John   III. Series
    658.8'5

ISBN 0 434 91288 3

Typeset by Deltatype Ltd, Ellesmere Port
Printed in Great Britain by
Redwood Burn Ltd, Trowbridge, Wilts

Contents

Preface   1

Introduction   3

1 The Problems Associated with Selling a Service   5

2 Reaching the Customers   46

3 Opening the Sales Interview   89

4 Benefit Selling   125

5 Dealing with Objections   149

6 Techniques for Closing the Sale   184

Model Answers   212

Index   264

Preface

'It's like trying to fill a leaky bucket with water.' This was the graphic way one sales director described his job when asked to do so at a recent seminar at Cranfield. Simplistic though it might be, many senior executives of service companies will readily understand why this particular analogy was used.

The 'leakage' occurs when existing customers order less, are lost to competitors, go out of business, or fail to re-order. This leakage is always there, as we will soon see if we examine our sales records over the last few years. Sometimes the leak is merely a dribble and hardly worth worrying about; but sometimes, for example when there are dramatic upheavals in the market place, as in times of economic uncertainty, the dribble of lost business can become something of a flood.

Quite rightly, most companies try to control and regulate the amount of business that leaks away from them each year by improving their customer service levels and by defending their market share more vigorously where appropriate. But, as we have seen, some loss is inevitable and so it is essential for the company continually to top up its bucket with new orders.

However, as we know from experience, just any order will not do, attractive though it might seem in the short term. What we need are those orders that are consistent with our marketing objectives and strategies. Only in this way will we secure the customer base that will be central to our survival and future success.

The importance of having a realistic and well-reasoned market-ing plan goes without saying. None the less, in many service companies it is the sales force that bears the brunt of making the plan come to life. In such companies, if it were not for the ability of the sales force to go out and win sales, then the marketing plan would be worthless.

This book therefore sets out to examine the whole sales process and thereby enable the reader to understand it better. Moreover, by working through the exercises and case studies that accompany this text, it will be possible to develop the skills needed to become a highly successful salesman*.

Malcolm H. B. McDonald
John W. Leppard
Cranfield School of Management
August 1988

* For simplicity 'salesman' and 'buyer' are referred to as masculine throughout, though it is appreciated that these might equally be feminine.

Introduction

Today, in the advanced industrialized nations, more people work in service industries than ever before. Moreover, as traditional manufacturing industries go into decline and new technological ones challenge to take their place, it is forecast that more and more service industries will develop and grow.

Looking around, there is clear evidence of this trend facing us on all sides. The office bureau services that jostle for attention in most towns, the computer programming and systems design consultancies that always seem to be advertising for staff as they expand. Yet it seems only a few years ago that they did not even exist.

Whatever service one might require, somebody somewhere seems to have anticipated the need with their 'specialist resourcing' type of enterprise.

However, it would be very wrong to conclude that all services are born out of technological developments. A great deal of manpower is still employed in those traditional bastions of the service industry such as banking, insurance, building societies and the legal professions.

But with the growth in the range and availability of services, inevitably competition becomes an inhibiting factor to the long-term success of a business.

As the industrialized countries face up to new economic realities, tradition and sentiment have less influence on business decisions than perhaps they did in the past.

What counts today is not having the best service but *selling the service* and the measure for success in doing this is quite stark and simple – if you don't sell, you don't survive.

We make no apologies for the fact that it is a simple book. It is about basic principles and procedures rather than about what some people refer to as 'advanced' selling techniques. It is our own view that the first prerequisite is to understand and practise the basics. If this is done professionally, there is no need for 'advanced' selling techniques.

1

The Problems Associated with Selling a Service

Overview

Selling a service can be a complex process and presents the salesman with difficulties not likely to be experienced by his counterpart selling a product.

A service does not lend itself to being specified in the same way as a product, as it does not have the same reproducible physical dimensions that can be measured. Thus with the purchase of any service there is a large element of trust on the part of the buyer. He can only be sure of the quality and performance of the service after it has been completed. There are other differences, and these too are examined.

A service can be supplied either to organizations or to private individuals. In both cases the sales process needs to be considered from the buyer's viewpoint. A series of buy phases can be seen to characterize all buying decisions. Moreover, the buyer is subjected to a range of pressures originating from both outside and inside his organization.

Whether the buyer represents a company (in which case several others might be involved in the decision-making) or just himself, it is possible to recognize different categories or types of purchase – referred to as buy classes.

By understanding the selling process from the buyer's point of view, the salesman is better equipped to conduct himself effectively. He will find it easier to identify the influential people in the buying process, to devise his sales strategy and to prepare himself for the different roles he will be expected to play.

Yet irrespective of all his planning and preparation, the salesman will still have to manage the many face-to-face interviews with buyers. Some of these he will take in his stride, but inevitably he will, from time to time, be confronted with the 'difficult' buyer.

It is possible to speculate about the various types of 'difficult' buyer and learn strategies for dealing with them.

For the salesman to conduct himself 'professionally' in his dealings with clients, not only must he behave correctly at all phases of the transaction, but he must also be aware of the potential pitfalls that await him if he does not observe conventional business ethics.

How selling a service differs from selling a product

What is so special about selling a service product, since the bucket analogy used in the introduction would be equally appropriate for a company selling a product as it is to one selling a service. How is it different? Perhaps this example will illustrate the nature of the difference.

Imagine a man who wants to buy a suit. He could walk into an outfitters and try various suits 'off-the-peg' until he found the one that was just right for him. Not only would he need to be satisfied with the colour, material and style, but in all probability he would carefully examine the stitching, how well the buttons did up and the overall cut of the suit. In effect he is buying a product made to a specification which could be physically checked and tested.

Now alternatively this same man could have approached a bespoke tailor to make his suit. He could certainly specify the colour, material and style that he required, but until the garment was actually completed he would have been trusting to luck that the finished product would meet his requirements to the full. The uncertainties of committing himself to this tailoring service would only be resolved in the fullness of time. This is a characteristic of the sales of all services.

1   *The element of trust*

It is never possible to know exactly what will be received until the service is rendered. The element of trust is dominant in all transactions.

Whereas a product can be measured against a specification or sample, a service can only be described; and we all know from experience that communication is not always as precise as we intend it to be.

For example, how could the efficiency of an estate agent be measured? By the speed at which a house was sold? By the lack of problems that occurred during the process of selling a house? By helping the vendor to achieve his asking price? Probably many other yardsticks spring to mind. The estate agent claiming the efficiency of his service might well be doing so on the basis of just one or two of these criteria.

Equally, his client's expectations of efficiency could well revolve around an entirely different set of criteria. Thus while the client buys and hopes for an efficient service, it is only at the completion of the transaction that he will actually be able to measure the degree to which it met his expectations.

But the element of trust is not the only distinguishing feature of a service.

2   *The product element of a service*

Just as with any product there is an element of service, such as delivery or after-sales service, so for any service there is a product element.

The market research organization provides a service which culminates in a product in the shape of a report for its client. The hairdresser provides his skills in order to arrive at the product, a stylish haircut. The portrait painter will require several sittings before he can deliver the framed painting. The architect will spend many weeks using his accumulated knowledge and skill preparing his product, a set of drawings.

It is important for the seller to be aware of the distinction between the service itself and the end product, because at the end of the day he has to be certain which of these the customer is buying. Is it the service, the special expertise that the seller can bring to bear on the customer's problem? Or is it the end result?

Clearly it has to be the former. The more an organization can demonstrate and earn a reputation for its particular expertise, the more customers will assume that the end outcome will be favourable for them. This aspect is obviously associated with the foregoing characteristic of a service, the element of trust. However, by trading on its expertise, the company selling a service distinguishes itself from those selling products in yet another way.

3   The salesman as part of the service

The product salesman, by definition, can never be part of his product. The product has its own physical dimensions and specifications which are self-contained and unique to it alone. At best the salesman will be seen as a representative of his company, conveying something of the image of that particular supplier.

When selling a service which, as we have already mentioned, cannot be specified in the same way as a product, it is the salesman's special expertise that is being sought by the prospective buyer. In that sense, the salesman becomes part of the 'package'. For example, the management training consultant who is persuading a company to use his services will undoubtedly run training courses in a distinctive way.

It will be this, just as much as the end result, that the company will be buying. Therefore throughout the sales process the salesman will be subjectively assessed by the buyer against all types of hidden criteria. 'Does he have the experience?' 'How will he get on with our managers?' 'Is he too theoretical?' All manner of these considerations will influence the buying decision and so, like it or not, the salesman becomes part of the service in a way that his counterpart selling a product could never be part of that product.

4 A service cannot be stored

Unlike products, services cannot be made in advance and stocked for selling 'off-the-shelf' at some later date.

We can see then that there are four ways in which selling a service can differ from selling a product:

1 The buyer purchases a service with a large element of hope or trust on his part, because a service cannot be specified in the same way as the physical dimensions of a product.
2 There can be a product element of the service which needs to be distinguished from the service itself.
3 The service salesman becomes part of the service, whereas the product salesman can never become part of the product.
4 Services are 'immediate', in the sense that they cannot be stocked.

Now these differences might be very important when it comes to selling some services. However, by and large, we believe that there are more similarities with selling products than differences. It is easy to see why. All sales situations are essentially interactions between the buyer, with his practical and psychological needs, and the salesman as he tries to respond to these.

Although ostensibly the meeting of the buyer and salesman is all about the purchase of a product or service, in fact the sales process is really about how well the salesman identifies the buyer's needs and establishes enough credibility for the buyer to commit himself with confidence to any specified transaction.

So let us switch our attention from the service itself to the sales situation. In practice this can take one of two forms, selling to an organization or selling to an individual.

Selling to an organization

Selling to an organization can sometimes prove to be a complex process because it is possible for a number of different people to become involved at the customer end. Although theoretically only one of these is the buyer, in practice he might not be allowed to make any decision to purchase until others with technical expertise or hierarchical responsibility have given their approval.

The personal authority of the buyer will to a large extent be governed by these factors:

1 *The cost of the service* – the higher the cost, the higher in the organization will the purchasing decision be made (see Figure 1).
2 *The 'newness' of the service* – the relative novelty of the service will pose an element of commercial risk for an organization. A new and untried proposition will require support at a senior management level, whereas a routine, non-risky service can be handled at a lower level.
3 *The complexity of the service* – the more complex the service offered, the more technical implications have to be understood within the client company. Several specialist managers might be required to give their approval before the transaction can be completed.

All those involved in the buying decision are known as the decision-making unit (D.M.U.), and it is important for the salesman

Level of expenditure	Level at which decision is taken			
	Board (collective)	Individual director	Departmental manager	Lower management or clerical
Over £50,000	88%	11%	2%	–
Up to £50,000	70%	25%	4%	Less than 0.5%
Up to £5,000	29%	55%	14%	2%
Up to £2,500	18%	54%	24%	4%
Up to £500	4%	31%	52%	14%

Figure 1 *Responsibility for financial expenditure*
        Source: How British Industry Buys, a survey conducted by Cranfield School of Management for *The Financial Times*, January 1984

to identify the D.M.U. in all current and prospective customer companies. Figure 2 gives some research findings which show how rarely salesmen reach all component members of the D.M.U.

A way of anticipating who would be involved in the decision-making processes in a company is to consider the sales transaction from the buyer's point of view. It has been recognized that the process can be split up into a number of distinct steps known as 'buy phases'.

Buy phases*

1 *Problem identification* – a problem is identified or anticipated and a general solution worked out. For example, the marketing planning department find that they have inadequate information about sales records and costs. They need better information made available on the computer.

2 *Problem definition* – the problem is examined in more detail in order to grasp the dimensions and hence the nature of the ultimate choice of solution. Taking our example further, investigation shows that the original software system was not devised with the current marketing planning requirements in mind. A new system is required which can also provide the option for the inclusion of other new data.

Number of employees	Average number of buying influences (the D.M.U.)	Average number of contacts made by salesman
0–200	3.42	1.72
201–400	4.85	1.75
401–1000	5.81	1.90
1000 plus	6.50	1.65

Figure 2 *Buying influences by company size*
         Source: McGraw-Hill

* This section of the text owes much to the original research conducted by the Marketing Service Institute in the USA under the guidance of Patrick J. Robinson.

3 *Solution specification* – the various technical requirements are listed and a sum of money is allocated to cover the cost of investing in new software.

4 *Search* – a search is made for potential suppliers. In this case, those with the capability of devising a 'tailormade' system to meet the above requirements.

5 *Assessment* – proposals from interested suppliers are assessed and evaluated.

6 *Selection* – a supplier is selected and probably final details are negotiated prior to the next step.

7 *Agreement* – a contract/agreement is signed.

8 *Monitoring* – the service is monitored in terms of meeting installation deadlines and performance claims.

If we happened to be running a computer programming service to industry, we could deduce from the above process that the D.M.U. at this company might well contain the following people: marketing planner, sales director, sales office manager, the company computer specialist, the company accountant, the company secretary and perhaps even the managing director, depending on the nature of the contract and the buyer. Sometimes the buyer might be one of those already listed and not exist as a separate role.

We could also speculate with some certainty that each of these people would need to be satisfied about different aspects of the efficiency of our programming service and we would need to plan accordingly. But more about that later.

For now, it is enough to recognize that when selling to an organization the person with the title of buyer is often unable to make important decisions on his own. Although he can be a useful cog in his company's purchasing machine, he is often not the free agent we might think he is.

Pressure on the buyer

When we purchase something for the home we know from our own experience how difficult it can sometimes be. Even if we are only buying a carpet, we have to agree whether or not it should be plain or patterned, what colour, what price, what quality, and so on. Even these considerations are clouded by issues such as whether the neighbours or relatives will think we are copying them, or whether we are being too chic, or too outrageous. The buying decision-makers in a typical company are faced with many more pressures than these. They stem from two origins: from outside the company; and from inside.

External pressures

These can be many and various and might include such issues as:

1 *The economic situation* – what will be the cost of borrowing? Are interest rates likely to rise or fall? Is it a good time to invest in a new service now? Is the market decline really over or should we wait for more signals of recovery?
2 *Political considerations* – how will government fiscal policy affect our business or that of our customers? Will proposed legislation have an impact on either us or our markets?
3 *Technology* – how are we as a company keeping up with technological developments? How does this new proposal rate on a technological scale? Is it too near the frontiers of existing knowledge? How long will it be before a whole new phase of technology supersedes this investment?
4 *Environmental considerations* – will this new service be advantageous to us in terms of energy conservation or pollution control? Does it present any increase in hazards to our workforce? Will we need more room to expand? Is such room available?
5 *The business climate* – how do our profit levels compare with those of companies in general and those in our type of business in particular? Are there material cost increases in the pipeline which could reduce our profits? Is the cost of labour increasing?

Any one of these could put pressure on the buying decision-maker – and these are only the external pressures.

Internal pressures

Within the company there can be another set of pressures, such as:

1 *Confused information* – it is often difficult to obtain the correct information to back up a buying decision. Either the information does not exist, or else it has not been communicated accurately from the specialist department. Sometimes it is not presented in a convenient form and leads to misunderstandings.
2 *Internal politics* – the relative status of individuals or departments can sometimes hinder the buying process. Personal rivalries or vested interests could create difficulties about priorities or standards. The 'politics' might entail non-essential people being involved in the decision-making process, thereby elongating the communication chain and slowing down decision-making.
3 *Organizational* – how the company is organized can affect the efficiency of its buying process. It is essential for everyone to be aware of their roles and levels of authority if they are to perform effectively.

Personal pressure

The buyer can be pressurized by a number of personal matters, some real, others imagined. He might be unsure about his role or how his colleagues accept his judgment. He might lack experience in the buying role and be unsure of how to conduct himself. He might prefer a quiet life and therefore be against change, preferring to continue his transactions with tried and tested suppliers – even if it can be clearly demonstrated that there are advantages in changing them. He might be naturally shy and not enjoy first meetings. He might find it difficult to learn new information about technical developments or special features of your particular service. He might feel he is too logical or perhaps not logical enough in his decision-making.

All of these pressures, both internal and external, have a profound bearing on the behaviour of the buyer, and if the salesman is to relate to the buyer he must try to understand them.

By way of summarizing this section on selling to industry, it can be demonstrated that the successful salesman needs to be aware of all these things when he approaches a buyer acting on behalf of an organization. He needs to know and understand:

1 The relative influence of the buyer in the context of the particular service being offered.
2 What constitutes the D.M.U. in the buying company.
3 How the buying process works.
4 The pressures on the buying decision-maker.

With this information in his possession he is in a better position to plan his work and conduct himself appropriately when face to face with the buying decision-maker(s). Exactly how this information is used will be covered later.

Selling to individuals

So far we have only looked at selling to organizations. Is selling to individuals any different? Well, to a large extent, no!

The individual will go through the same set of buy phases as the large organization, the only difference being that it all takes place in his head rather than being institutionalized as a system.

At first sight, the individual is the D.M.U., but be warned. If the service you offer is going to be relatively costly, as could be the case for specially designed house extensions, or demand a long-term level of commitment from the buyer, as in the case of insurance or private health schemes, then undoubtedly other people will be involved in the buying decision. A spouse, a partner or a friend will inevitably be the confidant that the buyer turns to when faced with such a big decision.

Except when the service is either inexpensive or routine, the concept of the individual buyer is something of a myth. It is easy to see why, for the individual buyer is subjected to almost as many pressures as his counterpart in an organization and he welcomes the opportunity to share the burden.

The only possible difference in selling to an individual rather than to an organization is likely to be in the area of what is perceived as the probable solution to the client problem.

In an organization, because of the number of people involved in the decision-making processes, the preferred solution will tend to be dictated by more logical and practical criteria. It is not difficult to understand why this should be so. Most managers will wish to demonstrate to their colleagues how rational they are and therefore will tend to present factual, reasoned arguments for proceeding with a proposed purchase.

The individual, without the psychological constraints of satisfying others, will respond to a problem in a more natural way. His choice of solution is just as likely to be made on the basis of feelings as logic. His ultimate choice is likely to be determined by a unique and personal combination of experience and personality type.

Buy classes

Whether or not the salesman is selling to an individual or to an organization, he can divide the decision-making process of his prospects into what are termed buy classes. There are three types of buy class:

1 *New buy* – in effect all the foregoing discussion has focused on the new buy category. It is here that those people who go to make up the D.M.U. are fully exercised as the buy phases unfold. It is in the new buy class that the needs of all decision-makers need to be met and influenced by the salesman. Not surprisingly, this takes

time and so it is not unusual for a lengthy period to elapse between the initial discussion and landing the contract.

2 *Straight re-buy* – once the salesman has had the opportunity to demonstrate how the service can help the customer, further purchases of the service do not generally require such a rigorous examination at all of the buy phases.

In fact, should the customer merely want a repeat purchase of the same service, then his only concerns are likely to be around issues such as: Has the price been held to the same level as before? Will the standard of the service be unchanged? Can it be provided at a specific time? Such issues can generally be resolved by negotiation with the buyer.

3 *Modified re-buy* – sometimes a modification in the service might be necessary. It might be that the supplier wants to up-date the service and provide better performance by using different methods or equipment. Alternatively, it could be the customer who calls for some form of modification from the original purchase. Whatever the origin, all or some of the buy phases will have to be re-examined, and again the salesman will have to meet and influence the relevant members of the D.M.U.

There are often advantages for a salesman to try and change a straight re-buy into a modified re-buy. They are two-fold:

1 A modified re-buy reactivates and strengthens the relationship with the various members of the customer's D.M.U.
2 The more closely a supplier can match his service to the customer's needs (and remember, this matching only comes about as a result of a mutual learning, as communication and trust develop between the supplier and the customer), the more committed the customer becomes to the service.

The higher the commitment the customer has to the particular service and the supplier, the more difficult it becomes for competitors to break in.

What does all this mean to the salesman?

So far in this chapter, all attention has been focused on the customer end of the buying transaction. We have looked at phases, D.M.U.s, buy classes and the pressure on buyers, be they individuals or representatives of organizations.

How does the salesman use this information to his advantage when selling his service?

Clearly, a good understanding of the above can assist the salesman in three important areas of his work:

1 Identifying the buyer
2 Preparing his sales strategy
3 Clarifying his role in complex sales situations.

Identifying the buyer

Recognizing that there is a D.M.U. is an important first step for the salesman, but having done this, it is essential to identify who actually has the power to make the purchase.

Failure to do so will result in much wasted time and frustration. No matter how persuasive the arguments for buying your service, if you are not reaching the key decision-maker then all your efforts might be in vain. Finding this person is too important to be left to chance and yet many salesmen fail to meet him. Sometimes they just have not done enough research about the company in order to get an accurate picture of how it operates, its personnel and the key issues that they are concerned with.

The Basic Research Checklist on page 29 will provide a number of ideas for remedying this particular failing.

Alternatively, many salesmen prefer to continue meeting their original contacts in the client company, the ones with whom they feel comfortable and have come to regard as friends, rather than extend their network of contacts. They fight shy of the risk of meeting the influential people in companies. Because many will hold senior positions, the thought of meeting them somehow seems a daunting prospect, especially to the complacent or ill-prepared salesman.

Yet many of these fears are groundless. There is no evidence that senior executives set out to be deliberately obstructive or use meetings to expose the salesman's possible inadequacies. In fact, quite the opposite appears to be true.

Certainly, they will be busy people and so will want discussion to be to the point and relevant. At the same time, they will be trying to get the best deal for their company and it is only natural that they should.

When meeting senior executives the salesman ought to follow this set of rules:

1 *Show respect* – and this does not mean being servile or sycophantic. Respect is best demonstrated by being punctual for the meeting, dressing appropriately and taking time to prepare *thoroughly* in advance.
2 *Address him and not his subordinates* – and make sure you get his name right.
3 *Be confident* – this is where thorough preparation helps because you will know how your service can match his needs and you will have all the necessary supporting information at your fingertips. You will also be clear about what you want to achieve from the meeting.
4 *Be business-like in your dealings with him* – never become over-friendly and do not waste his time.

Preparing a sales strategy

Preparation will be considered in more depth in Chapter 2, but for now it is enough to say that by understanding the buying process it becomes possible for the salesman to:

1 Recognize the buying situation and the stage it is at.
2 Plan his response to this accordingly.

3 Identify those people involved in the buying decision.
4 Calculate what benefits the service provides for each of these people.
5 Decide how best to influence these people and thereby influence the buying decision.
6 Attempt to convert straight re-buy situations into modified re-buys in such a way as to provide added benefits for the customer.

Although at first sight this might appear to be a fairly logical and straightforward process, in practice it is not, because in meeting and trying to influence the various people involved in the buying decision the salesman has to play a number of different roles.

The salesman's role

In order to achieve his objectives the salesman has to be ready to switch from one role to another. Fortunately, because most people in the D.M.U. have a quite specific and individual requirement, it is often possible for the salesman to act out one role at a time. Here are some of the most common roles.

Information officer

Research has shown that a very large number of companies rely on salesmen to keep them up-dated about new materials, developments in technology and many other aspects of their industry.

While some services might lend themselves to advertising, word-of-mouth still seems to be the most potent way of passing on information.

How the salesman prepares and equips himself for this role will have a profound bearing on his credibility and power to influence certain parts of the D.M.U.

Consultant

Often information is not enough. There are times when the salesman will be called upon to perform as a consultant; for example, to help resolve a problem of the client company, to help the buyer make a decision or to influence upwards in his own organization.

There are, however, some problems associated with this role:
— the consultant can too readily identify with a company problem and lose sight that his real goal was to be a salesman;
— in using his specialized knowledge and skill, the consultant can inadvertently obscure his potential to help behind a fog of jargon and technical expressions;
— the consultant might give ill-considered or over-hasty advice which could be damaging to his own credibility and the reputation of his company.

To fulfil the consultant role effectively the salesman must work at building up a relationship with the client which is based on trust and respect. He will not rush into providing solutions, but instead will ask a lot of questions designed to establish the exact nature of the client's needs.

He will listen carefully to the replies and only after analysing them will he recommend the action to be taken by the client. It follows that the salesman must have an excellent grasp of all the services that can be provided and a creative imagination to tailor them to fit the client's needs.

Salesman

An awful lot of salesmen (or should it be 'a lot of awful salesmen') get so enamoured with the previous two roles, they forget that their prime task is to sell a service.

Somehow, the more professional or technical the service, the more the salesman is trapped into thinking that he is revered for the specialist knowledge he has.

Unless he is in a seller's market, then he could not be more wrong.

Only a fortunate few companies can offer a unique service that cannot be copied or substituted. All the rest have to face up to competition. It is not surprising, then, that the old sales axiom still applies to most situations. 'When all things are equal, the orders usually go to the salesman with the greatest SELLING skills.'

It is for this reason that this book and the accompanying materials are so concerned with selling skills and how to improve them.

Negotiator

Sometimes even getting the customer to say yes is not enough. In these days of information technology and ever-increasing buyer sophistication, the client company might be more discriminating than ever before.

'Yes, I will buy your service if you will just agree to. . . .'

On hearing these words from a buyer, the unwary salesman is so pleased at getting the sale that he fails to grasp the significance of the end of the sentence. If he is not careful he is giving away extras to the buyer, in the shape of special conditions or terms, which can have the effect of wiping out any margins made on the sale.

Thus negotiation is quite different from selling. Negotiation begins when each party realizes that the other has something they want. The art of manoeuvring to get the best deal has sometimes been likened to getting a see-saw to balance. The relative weight and position of each party has a significant bearing on the tilt of the see-saw.

The salesman has to be able to exert influence on his side by knowing all about the relative costs and margins, his services, the effect of volume, price and sales mix on costs and also how competitors stand by comparison. Using this information intelligently he will perhaps stand a chance of negotiating successfully.

But it has to be recognized that negotiating skills are not the same as selling skills. There are many differences and one of the most obvious is the fact that the selling process follows a linear sequence, as this text discloses.

Negotiation follows no such pattern, indeed, there is evidence to show that good negotiators do not follow a linear pattern, but move from one issue to another in no particular pre-conceived sequence.

Whatever the role requirements, the successful salesman will be capable of recognizing what the situation requires and adopting the appropriate behaviour.

But there is yet another dimension of the sales situation with which the salesman has to cope . . . and that is being able to respond to the many and varied behaviours of the buyers he meets.

Coping with different types of buyer

Earlier in this chapter the sales process was examined from the buyer's viewpoint. It was evident from this that the buyer can be under quite a lot of pressure, some originating from outside the company, some from inside the company and some associated with the buyer's particular psychological make-up and personality.

Not surprisingly then, the salesman can find himself confronted with a whole range of buyer behaviours which for now we will classify as 'easy to cope with' to 'difficult to cope with'.

The better the salesman can handle the 'difficult buyers' the more effective he will become.

One might argue that every buyer is unique, an original personality in his own right. Yet in practice it does seem that difficult buyers fall into readily describable groups. The table on page 24 lists some stereotypes of difficult buyers and suggests how the salesman might respond to each one.

It does seem that the root cause of the buyer's difficult behaviour is fear — the fear of making a mistake, a decision, or owning up to where one stands.

Different types of difficult buyers and how to cope with them

Type	Description of buyer behaviour	Salesman's coping strategy
Friendly	Friendly and sympathetic with everything that is said. Nods his head and smiles a lot BUT is extremely difficult to pin down to make a decision.	Try not to get drawn into the 'friendship' but keep pushing to close the sale each time the buyer agrees. From time to time summarize all the agreements and then firmly but politely try to close.
Talkative	Talkers can fill up all the time in the sales interview. They interrupt, pontificate, side-track and waffle. At the end of all this, they say how interesting it was to meet you and recommend that you 'stay in touch'.	Timing is important. The talker has to pause at times, even if just to draw breath. Seize an opportune moment and interrupt in a courteous manner. For example, 'Yes, I agree with you there and that is precisely why we provide this new service.' Talkers are poor listeners, so be prepared to make your point more than once.
Silent	He says little but listens carefully to what is said. He might nod or give a non-commital 'uh uh' from time to time. The problem for the salesman is that he cannot gauge the buyer's interest in his proposal, know what objections there are or when to close.	The salesman must draw the buyer into the conversation by asking open-ended questions, i.e. those which cannot be answered by 'Yes' or 'No'. For example, '. . . Well, that's how we see it, but I would be most interested to hear your views Mr Smith.' If there is a silence after asking a question, do NOT break it. Uncomfortable as it may seem, just sit and wait for the buyer's reply.

Prevaricator	Talks on a grand scale and is full of promises. The big order is just around the corner but somehow it never seems to materialize.	There are two possibilities here: 1 The buyer is just leading you on, in which case call his bluff by asking for an interview/pilot order which will give the company a chance to evaluate the quality of your service. 2 A big order is in the offing, in which case get down to talking details (the genuine prevaricator will not want to do this) and check who else might be involved in the buying decision.
Mule	Characterized like the animal with stubbornness. Once his mind is made up, nothing will change it. Rational argument or impassioned appeal will fall on deaf ears. Afraid of appearing weak, this type of buyer would prefer to make a wrong decision than to climb down. Indeed, any implied criticism of his decision will almost certainly wreck all chances of getting an order.	Try delaying the opportunity for the buyer to make up his own mind on the total package. Angle your presentation so that you are encouraging him to think in a particular way. For example, 'We find that the more far-sighted companies prefer this particular aspect of our service because it is the least disruptive way of introducing new control systems.'
Pompous	The pompous buyer is full of his own importance and power (which is sometimes nothing like as much as he would have you believe). He is motivated very much by status issues and recognition from superiors. Can be self-opinionated and sarcastic (as a defence mechanism).	The last thing the salesman should attempt to do, no matter how high the temptation, is to prick the balloon of pomposity. Always look for an opportunity to give credit where it is due. For example, 'I do like the way you have the open plan office laid out'. But never by fawning. Above all, stick to facts in your presentation – facts are neutral, whereas your opinions will be unlikely to better his.

Experienced

The experienced buyer has seen it all before. He might play the odd 'game' with you, just for fun to break his routine or to test if you are on your mettle. For example, he might 'play' at being a silent buyer to see how you react. He will see through poorly-reasoned arguments, but equally he will recognize a good presentation when he sees one.

Respect his experience by preparing your presentation and ensuring that all supporting materials will be on hand.

Never try to bluff this buyer. Be honest with him and even be prepared to seek his advice on matters where his wisdom can help.

Inexperienced

Everybody was inexperienced at their job at one time. This buyer will be wanting to demonstrate he can cope, but be worried about making mistakes.

He will probably not have all the necessary company facts at his disposal. In his early days he will probably only be entrusted with the more routine purchase.

Remember, his company recognizes that he is capable enough to be given this problem, so he is not an idiot. Treat him with respect and do not talk down to him.

Take the pressure off him by suggesting the 'agenda' for the meeting. For example, 'How about if I quickly tell you something about my company. Then you tell me why you are interested in our service. After that we can discuss where our services will best meet your needs'. Take the opportunity to teach him all about your company and its services.

Shy

Shyness manifests itself in various ways – by being silent, by nervous fiddling with items on the desk and by avoiding eye contact. Together or singly these behaviours can mislead the salesman into thinking he is boring the buyer. In an attempt to be more stimulating, the salesman deviates from his planned presentation and fails to cover the key points.

Shyness is not a measure of lack of experience or intelligence. It is a personal characteristic in the same way as height, weight, colour and shape. The salesman should use involved strategies like open-ended questions and working out calculations together. Such cooperation could help to overcome much of the shyness.

Busy

Their phones are always ringing, people keep coming into their office with questions or pieces of paper. It is barely possible to start a conversation before it is interrupted.

Sometimes the buyer is genuinely busy but equally some buyers are just ill-organized or enjoy working under these conditions.

There are three possible ways of coping:

1 Be impressed that the buyer can function under such pressure, e.g. 'How do you manage to cope with all this going on?' The buyer might then perhaps begin to talk about his problems and relax enough to spare the time for the presentation.

2 Check if you have called at an unusually busy time and arrange another meeting, e.g. early morning before work normally starts or late in the day.

3 Confront the buyer for his lack of respect towards you – because after all you have a job to do as well. Remember you do not sell anything while you are just waiting around cooling your heels. Be sure to do this as politely as possible, since you will want to try to re-arrange the meeting without such interruptions next time.

Ethical considerations

In the course of conducting his business the salesman must be aware of the various constraints of his actions. Some of these might be laid down by a trade association or some other sort of regulating body, others fall into the category of custom and practice, or as often as not, personal conscience.

Advertising and promotion

The governing bodies of some types of service industries do not allow any form of advertising on the part of their members. Other bodies might allow a modest amount of advertising as long as it conforms to certain rigidly controlled standards.

The salesman must be clear about what is acceptable for the service he offers, because it can severely hamper the means at his disposal for making contact with prospective clients. It might also impose limitations on how much he might say, for example, in reference to his successes in other client companies.

Entertaining

Most salesmen will at one time or another entertain a buyer, or vice-versa. Invariably, this takes the form of a modest lunch or even sometimes a dinner together.

Such activities might be useful in cementing the friendship between the salesman and the buyer, or in providing them with an opportunity to talk quietly away from the interruptions of the office. However, it has to be recognized that it is extremely rare for such entertaining to influence the final contract.

Sometimes, for example, when a new service is being launched, there might be a more lavish level of entertainment when buyers are invited to some exotic venue. But generally speaking, these sorts of functions are not arranged by the salesmen but by a senior director.

As a general rule, entertainment should be kept in perspective. After all, another calorie-packed meal is not a particularly attractive proposition for the executive who eats out regularly and is desperately trying to reduce weight.

The skilled salesman sells his service on the basis of its quality and what it can do for his customer.

Bribery

In most countries bribery, of course, is illegal as a means of influencing a deal.

But even if this were not the case, it must be remembered that the whole reputation and livelihood of the buyer is based on his success in obtaining the best possible service for his company. Furthermore, he is expected to justify his choice against a set of mainly logical criteria agreed by his company. Is it likely he would choose the second best when he is under such strict security?

Liability to the customer

The supplier of a service will have both legal and moral obligations to see that the service matches up to its description.

Therefore it is essential that the salesman does not make any claims for the service which cannot be subsequently substantiated or fulfilled.

Basic research checklist

The salesman selling his service to organizations should find out as much as possible about his potential customers.

Here are some suggestions for the types of basic research information that would be useful for the salesman. It will be important to ensure that this information is kept up-to-date.

1   The company

– what sort of company is it and what is its business?
– how big is it?
– is it privately owned or part of a group?
– is the company profitable?
– is it expanding or contracting?
– what dealings have you had with this company in the past?
– does it have a traditional or modern image?

2   Its products and markets

– what does the company make?
– (alternatively) what is the range of services it offers?

– what is the company's standing in its markets? (e.g. is it a leader?)
– are its markets expanding or contracting?
– are new products/services being developed?
– is the current business climate supportive or damaging to either the company or its customers?
– who are its strongest competitors?

3   Its personnel

– who is responsible for buying your type of service?
– what sort of person is he?
– who else is likely to be involved in the buying decision?
– what do you know about them?
– who has the real power?

4   Its systems

– how does its purchasing system work?
– who are the key administrators of the system?
– how does its invoicing system work (to facilitate the financial transaction)?

5   Its suppliers

– has it used your type of service before?
– who are the current suppliers?
– how have they performed?
– what is the range and price of the service provided?

   Not all of this information will be readily available, but it should be possible to assemble most of it by using the following sources:
– your own company records of previous transactions;
– other salesmen;
– other customers;
– telephone enquiries to the company;

— informal discussions with gatekeepers, receptionists, van drivers, etc.;
— national and local newspapers;
— trade press;
— the company's own brochures and promotional material;
— Chambers of Trade;
— trade directories;
— exhibition catalogues;
— Kompass;
— Kelly;
— Yellow Pages;
— Extel Cards;
— Trade Association;
— etc., etc.

Application questions

1 How does the current range of your sales activity split in terms of:
   — new buys?
   — straight re-buys?
   — modified re-buys?
   Has this pattern changed over the past two years? If it has been stable over this period, are there any signals that suggest this pattern might be starting to change now? What scope do you have to obtain new business by convincing customers that existing straight re-buys should become modified re-buys?

2 Which sources of information do you find to be most useful when you are researching potential customers? Which sources of information do you find least useful? Could your company provide you with more helpful information when you do this research?

3 Does your sales literature give you sufficient information on

which to base discussions with prospective buyers? Are there any
ways that your sales literature could be improved? How?

4 What do buyers see as the most important pressures on them
from:
– the environment?
– their company? (if an organizational buyer)
Is there anything you or your company can do to reduce these
pressures?

5 Consider the various roles you might be expected to play –
information officer, consultant, salesman and negotiator. Which
of these roles do you find most difficult? What could your
company do to make the role easier? What can you do to improve
your performance in the role?

Exercises

On the pages which follow are exercises designed to reinforce some
of the key messages in this chapter. You will probably find it useful
to work through them, but before you do, here are two important
points to remember.

1 *Work at your own pace* – everybody has a different speed for
reading and there are no prizes for finishing quickly. If anything
crops up which you don't fully understand, be prepared to re-
read the text and seek clarification. Complete each exercise
before moving on to the next one.

2 *Model answers* – these are provided at the end of the book. It
must be appreciated that for some of the exercises precise
answers cannot be given. Therefore those provided are intended
to be illustrations rather than prescriptions to be followed
slavishly. They will however give you some yardstick against
which to measure your own solutions.

Further exercises are provided after each chapter of this book.

We hope you enjoy working through them and can relate them to your day-to-day work.

Exercise 1.1:   'True or false' quiz

The following statements are either true or false. Indicate your answer with a tick in the appropriate box on the right hand side of the page. When you have completed this quiz, check the text again to find out if you have answered the questions correctly.

		True	False
1	In buying products and services a high element of trust is present in all transactions.	☐	☐
2	Modified re-buys require little re-examination of the buy phases.	☐	☐
3	The greatest difficulty in selling services is the fact that there is never an end product for the customer.	☐	☐
4	In the long run the successful salesman is the one who exploits his existing network of customers to the full rather than goes chasing after new ones.	☐	☐
5	When selling a service the salesman's special expertise becomes part of the sales offer.	☐	☐
6	Emotion plays a greater part of the decision making process of the individual than in that of the organization, which tends to be more rational.	☐	☐
7a	The salesman needs to get the buyer in a company on his side.	☐	☐
7b	If he achieves that he is virtually home and dry.	☐	☐
8	With similar services the orders usually go to the salesman with the greatest selling skills.	☐	☐
9	Since there is a lot of uncertainty involved in buying a service, 'entertainment' can influence the placing of a contract.	☐	☐

10 Negotiation, unlike selling, does not follow a linear
sequence. Good negotiators often move from issue
to issue in random fashion. ☐   ☐

Turn to page 212 to check your answers.

Exercise 1.2: *What needs do you want your job to satisfy?*

In Chapter 1, we looked at the 'sales triangle' and saw that it was
comprised of three quite separate and distinct 'corners':

1 The salesman . . . with all his needs and pressures.
2 The product . . . and all its attributes.
3 The buyer . . . with all his needs and pressures.

This exercise is designed to focus attention on the salesman and
to learn something about 'what makes him tick', in other words,
what he is looking for from the job of 'salesman'. Clearly personal
motivation is a key contributing factor when considering how a
salesman performs.

Complete Part 1 before turning to Part 2. Only when you have
completed Part 3, turn to page 213 for an interpretation of your
results.

Part 1 *Motivation questionnaire*

The following statements have the seven possible responses as
shown . . .

0	1	2	3	4	5	6

Strongly disagree		Slightly disagree		Slightly agree		Strongly agree
	Disagree		I am undecided		Agree	

Please respond to every one of the thirty statements given below
by writing your response score in the box for that statement. For

example, if you slightly disagree with statement 1, you would 'score' it 2.

1   I feel uncomfortable because I believe too high a proportion of my earnings are dependent upon commission from sales. □

2   A clear job description would be helpful if I am to know what is expected of me. □

3   I like to be reminded from time to time how the company is performing and what we must do to stay competitive. □

4   My manager should pay a good deal of attention to the physical conditions under which we work, e.g. suitable car, back-up services, etc. □

5   The manager ought to work hard to develop a friendly atmosphere among the salesforce. □

6   Individual recognition for above standard performance means a lot to me. □

7   Indifferent management can often 'bruise' a salesman's feelings and damage team spirit. □

8   I want my real skills and capacities put to use in the daily work. □

9   Anything the company can do to help its salesmen e.g. improved pensions, better training and development, are important factors in an employee satisfaction programme. □

10   Almost every sales job can be made more challenging and stimulating. □

11   I want to give my best in everything I do. □

12   Management could show more interest in the salesforce by encouraging more 'get-togethers' and 'out of hours' social events. □

13   Pride in one's work is an important reward for a salesman. □

14   I want to be able to think of myself as 'the best' in my job. □

15   The quality of informal relationships in the sales team is important. □

16   I believe my sales territory is really too large to be managed comfortably. □

17   I believe that for me to have 'visibility' with higher management is an important factor in being successful. □

18   I would generally like to schedule my own work and to get on with the job with the minimum of supervision. □

19   Job security is important for me. □

20   Having well-designed sales aids, brochures etc. is important to me. □

21 Overall I work unsociable hours or am away from home too much, which I find to be dissatisfying. ☐

22 I dislike a working day/week which is fraught with uncertainty. ☐

23 I believe that it is important for a sales job to serve a useful social purpose. ☐

24 A job in sales is a good way to establish a prestigious life style. ☐

25 Sales work, because it involves meeting people, enables me to develop and grow as a person. ☐

26 I have to be prepared to make, and enjoy making, decisions in my work. ☐

27 There is always a hard pace and pressure in my job, which overall I do not enjoy. ☐

28 Appraisal meetings with my manager are threatening and not very constructive. ☐

29 I believe that sales training can have the effect of causing a salesman to lose his individuality. ☐

30 Being a salesman enables you to meet lots of people and establish many worthwhile relationships with friendly customers. ☐

Part 2 Motivation questionnaire

Transfer your scores from Part 1 as follows:

Add your scores for statement numbers

1	4	16	20	21	27	A ☐

Write this total in Box A

Add scores for statement numbers

2	3	9	19	22	28	B ☐

Write this total in Box B

Add scores for statement numbers

5	7	12	15	23	30	C ☐

Write this total in Box C

Add scores for statement numbers

| 6 | 8 | 14 | 17 | 24 | 29 |

Write this total in Box D

Add scores for statement numbers

| 10 | 11 | 13 | 18 | 25 | 26 |

Write this total in Box E

Part 3   Motivation questionnaire

Now enter your box scores from Part 2 on to this chart using the method outlined in the example given below.

Score	0	3	6	9	12	15	18	21	24	27	30	33	36
Box E													
Box D													
Box C													
Box B													
Box A													

Example

If your score for Box A was 20, draw a vertical line corresponding to the 20 position and then shade the Box A row up to your score line.

        0   3   6   9   12 15 18 21 24 27 30 33 36

| Box A |

20

Use this procedure for recording all of your box scores.

Note: Now turn to page 218 for an interpretation of your results.

Exercise 1.3:   Customer analysis

Chapter 1 describes how the buying process can be split up into eight buy phases.

1   Problem identification – general solution.
2   Problem definition – more detail is extrapolated to refine the solution.
3   Solution specification.
4   Search for suppliers.
5   Supplier proposals evaluated.
6   Supplier selected.
7   Contract agreed.
8   Monitoring of service.

The chapter also looked at buy classes, D.M.U.s and pressures on buyers. Clearly a salesman needs a lot of knowledge about a customer if he is to identify the buyers correctly and prepare a sales strategy. This knowledge is only obtainable by research, e.g. developing your intelligence about the customer. The objective of this exercise is to help you to learn how to do this.

Step 1

Choose an important customer or target business sector and use this to practise your customer analysis. The Basic Research Checklist on page 29 should provide much of the information you need in order to continue to Step 2.

Step 2

Use the customer analysis form on pages 40 and 41 to identify the people involved at each stage and the different factors they might consider. These factors can be identified by numbers placed in the appropriate boxes. Examples of different factors which may be considered are listed at the bottom of the form. But please recognize that you can add to these.

Once this has been accomplished you should be in a position of knowing about your major customer or target industry.

(a)   Which managers influence and take buying decisions.
(b)   What information is appropriate for each one concerning your service.

Also you will have:

(c)   A technique for analysing *all* your customers and producing similar matrix forms for your customer record file.

Exercise 1.4:   *Dealing with difficult buyers*

Part 1

Step 1:   Cut some pieces of paper to roughly playing card size and on each piece write the name of one type of difficult buyer listed in Chapter 1 e.g. pompous. If you can think of others which were not listed then make a 'card' for them also.

Step 2:   Take the set of cards depicting the various types of 'difficult' buyers, shuffle them and then place the pack of cards face down in front of you.

Step 3:   Have notepaper and pen available. Take the top card from the shuffled pack and turn it over, face upwards. Respond to this card by writing down on the paper how you would typically handle this type of buyer.

Step 4:   Repeat the above process until all the cards in front of you have been tackled in a similar manner.

Step 5:   Compare your notes with those given in Chapter 1.

Note: If there is not a very high level of agreement between your notes and the book, study this section before proceeding.

Customer analysis form

Salesman: _____

Service(s): _____

_____

Date of analysis: _____

Date of reviews: _____

Buy phase	Board	Committee	Director	General Manager	Design/ Engin-eering
	Main or sub-sidiary	Name	Title Name	Name	Name
1 Recognizes needs or problem and works out general solution.					
2 Works out characteristics and quantity of what is needed.					
3 Prepares detailed specification.					
4 Searches for and locates potential sources of supply.					
5 Analyses and evaluates tenders, plans, etc.					
6 Selects supplier.					
7 Places order.					
8 Checks and tests.					

How to use the matrix

Opposite are a number of typical decision-forming factors which will be considered by different managers at various stages of the buying process. Others can be added. To use the matrix, indicate in each management function and each stage of the buying process at which they are likely to be involved, those factors they will take into account in arriving at a decision. Check that the managers concerned have the appropriate information on your product and the method of communicating this information to the manager is effective.

Customer: _____

Address: _____

_____

Buy classes: New buy ☐ Straight re-buy ☐   Modified re-buy ☐

Telephone No. (STD code _____) _____

Production	Sales marketing	Research and development	Finance and accounts	Purchasing	Data processing	Other	Other
Name	Name	Name	Name	Name	Name	Name	Name

Factors for consideration
1 = Price
2 = Performance characteristics
3 = Availability
4 = Back-up service
5 = Reliability of supply firm
6 = Other user experience
7 = Guarantees and warranties
8 = Payment terms, credit and discount
9 = Past purchases prestige/image etc.

Part 2

Step 1: Take all the cards and lay them out in a row in front of you in the following manner:

(a)   The least difficult buyer card is placed on the extreme left.
(b)   The most difficult buyer card is placed on the extreme right.
(c)   All other cards are positioned in terms of 'difficulty' between these two end positions.

Example

| A | B | C | E | H | J |

Buyer least difficult for me

| | | D | F | I |

| | | G | |

Buyer most difficult for me

In this example Card B is relatively easy to deal with, Cards EFG are similar and moderately difficult, whereas H and I are clearly at the most difficult end with J.

Step 2: When you are satisfied that the cards are laid out to your complete satisfaction, relative to each other, make a note of their position.

Step 3: Analyse the 'buyers' at the difficult end of your layout and answer the following questions:

(a)   What is it that distinguishes the difficult buyers from the less difficult buyers?
(b)   Do these distinguishing features say something about
  • You? e.g. your lack of experience, confidence, etc.
  • The buyer? e.g. his insensitivity, etc.
  • The buyer's situation?
(c)   What steps should you take to become more effective in dealing with these 'difficult' buyers in terms of:

- Your preparation for such sales meetings?
- Your face-to-face interview skills?
- Your longer term personal development?
- Anything else?

Note: Make a note of the key issues that emerge from this analysis.

Follow up activity

See if you can get a friend or colleague to 'role play' one of the difficult buyers and test out how your improvement strategy seems to work.

Exercise 1.5:   The easy sale

Read this case study and make notes about the following questions:

1   Should David Brown feel so pleased?
2   What were the critical parts of the interview?
3   How might the interview have been handled differently?
4   What key piece of information is still unknown to David Brown?

David Brown could hardly believe it. There he was in full spate talking about the benefits of Acme Engineering's tool repair service. Jeff Gregory, the buyer facing him, was listening attentively to everything David said. The meeting was going so well.

'Surely this can't be the difficult Mr Gregory we have been trying to pin down for the last four years,' thought David to himself, 'he seems such a reasonable chap'.

David Brown had been with Acme for some time. It was his first job as a sales representative. Before this he had worked in a design office dealing with customer enquiries.

It was with some surprise that David had landed the appointment to meet Mr Gregory. His predecessor's file notes on Victoria Presses had not been hopeful. It seemed that a competing tool repair service had been successful in meeting all their needs. Whenever Gregory had been approached in the past, he had let it be known in no uncertain terms that he was happy with his current arrangements and did not wish to be pestered by Acme sales representatives.

Something had obviously changed.

As David came to the end of his presentation, he looked eagerly across the desk at Gregory. The buyer's face was impassive, but his sharp, twinkling eyes betrayed the shrewd intelligence that had made him so successful in his long career in buying.

'What do you think about our service, then?' said David to break the uncomfortable silence. 'I reckon that we take some beating.'

'Mmm,' grunted Gregory thoughtfully, 'but you do seem to be a bit on the expensive side.'

David Brown was half expecting Gregory to say something like this and had already planned his reply, after all he did have some discretion over the prices he could charge.

'Well, I could give you a 25 per cent discount. That makes it a very attractive proposition, don't you think?'

Gregory didn't reply immediately. He seemed suddenly interested in something on the ceiling and he leaned back in his chair staring upwards.

Silence again, except for a slight noise that Gregory's fingers made as he drummed them on the pencil he was holding between his long, tapering fingers.

David became conscious of the ticking of the wall clock, it seemed to get louder and louder. The thought of losing such a big customer as Victoria Presses was beginning to worry him. Again he broke the silence.

'Well, Mr Gregory, because you are such a prestigious company I think I can manage to give you a further discount of 5 per cent. But nothing more.'

At this Jeff Gregory came alive again. His eyes met David's and he looked pleased. 'I think that offer is pretty reasonable.' He leaned forward, 'But perhaps we can just clear up one or two points.'

'Certainly,' said David barely listening as the euphoria of getting the business with Victoria started taking over his brain. He could already imagine telling his sales manager about the deal. How could he celebrate? I know, I'll take the wife out to dinner tonight.

Gregory's voice brought him back from his triumphant musing. 'Certainly,' he said again, 'Points you say? What did you have in mind?'

'Well', said Gregory, 'as you know we do have another plant in the North. You will be able to offer them the same service as down here, won't you?'

'Yes,' replied David, although he was beginning to wonder if they did have other customers situated near Victoria Presses' northern plant. Still, he thought, with motorways and a fast van, collection and delivery shouldn't be a problem.

'Oh! And another thing,' continued Gregory, 'Most of our big orders are for export contracts. We have to meet very strict deadlines, so we can't afford to be let down by your lot if we get an urgent tool repair job. We would have to insist that there is a penalty clause if you hold up our production.'

David wasn't too sure about this, but after all he had landed the contract, it would be silly to spoil it all over a mere detail. 'That should be all right Mr Gregory,' and they shook hands on the deal.

As he drove away David Brown felt pleased that he had done a good morning's work. 'I think I'm going to enjoy being a sales representative,' he thought. 'It isn't as difficult as people make out.'

Back in his office Jeff Gregory stood up, stretched, and walked over to the window. He smiled to himself as he watched David Brown's car drive away. He too felt most satisfied.

When you have answered the questions about this case study, compare them with the comments provided on page 222.

2

Reaching the Customers

Overview

The successful salesman recognizes that he has to maximize the time he has actually selling to customers and at the same time minimize the non-productive parts of his day such as travelling, waiting and spending time with the 'wrong' contacts.

Because of his need to have regular coverage of his territory, balance his time between current and potential customers, provide the right level of service to a range of different-sized and geographically spread companies, the salesman must develop a territory plan.

The investment in time spent on planning pays off later when the salesman comes to arrange appointments with those he has identified as prospects. Typically, he will reach these people by telephone to arrange an appointment. Often the telephone call will be preceded by a 'selling' letter.

In making the 'phone call the salesman will have prepared, in the sense of knowing whom he wishes to contact and the reason for doing so. He will have a lever for the call to arouse the buyer's interest and he will know how to close the call with the arrangements for an appointment.

Sometimes switchboard operators, secretaries and others will act as a 'protective screen' for the buyer. The successful salesman needs to know how to overcome such obstacles.

Even when he makes contact with the buyer, he still has to know how to counter objections like 'I'm too busy to see you' or 'We don't need your service'. There are special techniques and approaches that can help the salesman.

Finally, there is the business of fixing an appointment at a time of day most appropriate for the buyer, but in such a way that the salesman is really in control of his daily work plan and therefore keeps unnecessary travelling to a minimum.

Reaching the customers

In the previous chapter we looked at the selling process in some detail and considered various ways the salesman could overcome the problems associated with selling a service. Particular attention was paid to buy phases, recognizing the decision making unit, and to collecting basic market research. We saw that this information helps us to uncover who is really the buyer in any prospective client company.

However, identifying the buyer is one thing, actually reaching him is quite another. The theme of this chapter is that the salesman operating in the field must run his territory as a 'business' and in doing so should endeavour to do two things:

1 Maximize his contact with customers and hence improve his chances of realizing the sales potential of his territory.
2 Minimize his costs by reducing unproductive areas of his work such as travelling time, waiting and time spent at meetings with the 'wrong' people.

Obvious though these points might be, they will not happen by chance. The salesman will have to develop a 'business' plan for his territory and consciously strive to manage his time more effectively if these two aims are to become reality.

Yet, to mention the word 'plan' to many salesmen can be likened to waving the proverbial red rag at a bull. To them planning is seen as a straitjacket, the antithesis of what they claim to be the secret of success – the ability to be flexible, to be able to respond to situations and opportunities as they arise.

What then might have caused them to take this viewpoint?

Some difficulties of planning

The advocates of non-planning will probably give these examples to support their case that planning doesn't work in practice:

Sudden requests

'You plan your work for the next week and then the 'phone rings and it's either the office saying that you've got to see so-and-so tomorrow, or else it's a customer saying that they have to see you about something important.'

Understandably, this salesman is a bit peeved that the time he has spent trying to plan has apparently been wasted by sudden requests, thrust upon him by external forces beyond his control.

He now sees himself being forced to 'phone customers to break hard won appointments in order to accommodate these new requests.

Complaints

Like sudden requests, a complaint can crop up at any time. The conscientious salesman recognizes the importance of responding to the customer as quickly as possible and yet in doing so, sees his erstwhile plan falling apart.

Unknown interview time

'You can't plan with any certainty how long you will be with a customer. After all, it would be daft to limit the meeting to some artificial time constraint planned in advance. If the meeting is going well, you will naturally want to keep it going and get as much out of it as you can.'

Administrative demands

From time to time the salesman is faced with administrative demands to which he is obliged to respond. For example, the marketing department wants to obtain certain information that can only come from the field sales staff. Such situations can cut across any planning the salesman might have been attempting to implement.

Territory planning is further complicated by issues such as:
– different call frequencies and requirements of different customers;
– difficulties of travel and parking, especially in large cities;
– the need to find new business and yet not lose touch with existing customers;
– the uneven geographical spread of existing and potential customers.

Taken together, these points suggest that territory planning is not quite as simple as some people might have one believe. But is it enough evidence to justify not planning? We do not think so.

What the above seems to point out very clearly is not the need to abandon planning, but the need for planning to be flexible and to be capable of accommodating the inevitable unexpected request.

In fact, territory planning is essential because only by planning will the salesman achieve:
– regular coverage of his territory;
– reduced travel time (see Figure 3).
– the right coverage of each market segment;
– improved customer relations;
– exposure to more sales situations;
– the right balance between existing customers and new prospects.

Breakdown of a salesman's daily activity

One major company used work study techniques to establish how the salesmen used their time. This is what they discovered. Similar

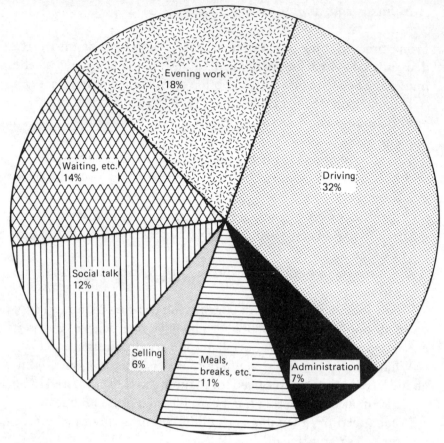

Figure 3

studies in other companies to a large extent support these findings.

How to plan

There are various ways to set about planning a territory. Some rely on very accurate measurement about how salesmen spend their time. Others are far less sophisticated and draw heavily on practical experience. But whatever the system used, certain basic principles need to be applied.

The method we describe here produces a workable plan and incorporates these basic principles.

1 Classify customers and potential customers according to their business potential

It is best not to have more than three or four categories of customer, for example:

Actual or high potential:	this might be for, say, levels over £100,000 of business
Actual or medium potential:	then this becomes between £50,000–£100,000 of business
Actual or low potential:	under £50,000 of business

However, instead of using words like high, medium and low, which could be somewhat emotive if the customer got to hear about them by accident, many companies classify their customers by letter grades.

Thus the levels of business given above might be designated grades A, B and C.

2 Map the territory

It is useful to prepare a large scale map of the territory. If no such map exists, be prepared to cut and join several maps until you have an area map to meet your requirements.

It is a good idea to mount your map on to a board and to cover it with clear plastic. Not only does this protect the map, but it also gives you the facility to use felt pens, for example to experiment with individual route plans. Afterwards, the pen marks can be wiped off with a damp cloth.

3 Pinpoint the customers

Using coloured map pins to represent each customer, build up a pictorial representation of the sales territory on the map. Remember to use different coloured pins to indicate whether or not the customer is an existing or a potential one. Also use different coloured pins to signify the customer category you have allocated them.

The map will now be a fair representation of all the places where visits are required.

4   Estimate the workload

On the assumption that a salesman can work for something like 235 days of the year (i.e. a full year, less annual leave, weekends and bank holidays) calculate how many calls will be possible in the year.

This will be the *average* number of calls possible in a day, multiplied by 235. For example, if our experience tells us that it is feasible to visit six customers per day, then the maximum possible visiting time will be in the order of 1410 calls per year.

5   Establish call rates for customer grades

With a known number of calls at one's disposal, it becomes a relatively simple matter to allocate how many calls can be made to existing and potential grade A, grade B and likewise grade C customers. Generally, it will be useful to involve the field sales manager in this exercise, because rarely do things balance out straight away. What is most likely, is that there will be a need for some adjustment to call frequencies until the arithmetic is correct. Thus the final figures, using the example above, should look something like this:

No. of class A customers × their call frequency =
No. of class B customers × their call frequency =
No. of class C customers × their call frequency =

$$\text{Total} \quad \underline{1410}$$

6 *Divide up the territory*

The whole territory now needs to be divided into a number of sub-areas, each sub-area having a similar annual total number of calls.

Each sub-area is in turn divided into a number of daily routes, each route being chosen to minimize the travel needed to visit prospects within that route. (See Figures 4 and 5.)

It is a good idea to try to make each daily route such that it has a mix of customer classes but overall contains a similar business potential. In this way, a salesman can readily monitor his performance because by and large he ought to achieve similar results each day.

In fact, achieving consistent results motivates salesmen better than the peaks and troughs pattern of results that is the typical outcome of poorly planned routes.

It is also considered good practice not to visit the same area always on the same day. This is because some important contacts might never be available on particular days. For example, one company might always have its board meetings on Thursdays, thus directors will always be too busy to see the salesman.

Organizing the sales territory

Stage 1

Divide the territory into sub-areas, each having a similar annual total number of calls (Figure 4(a)). Note that each sub-area can be a different size when the territory is divided on this basis.

Stage 2

Divide each sub-area up into daily routes to minimize the travel (Figure 4(b)).

Minimizing the travel

Some salesmen prefer to drive out to the furthest customer first while they are fresh and then work their way back home. They find this motivating, knowing that they will not be faced with a long

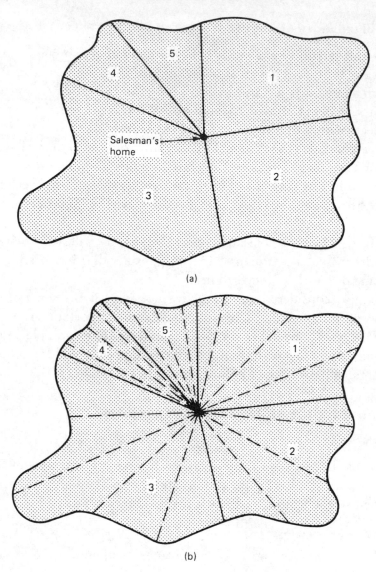

(a)

(b)

Figure 4   *(a) Stage 1*
            (b) Stage 2

drive at the end of the day. Such a route would be Home – D – E – C – B – F – A – Home (see Figure 5).

This approach is frequently not the shortest journey. What is often better is to follow a circular route such as Home – F – E – D – C – B – A – Home. It is invariably shorter and yet still offers the inducement of working back towards home. When you plan your daily routes, consider the circular trip. Measure it on your territory map and compare the saving.

HOME

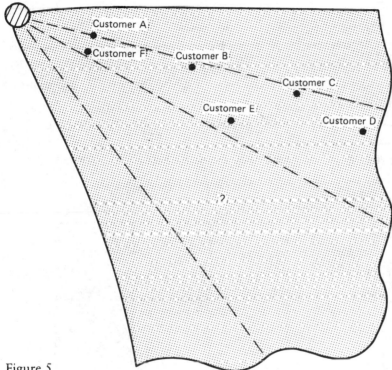

Figure 5

As a routine, it is often useful to compile a weekly visit programme by selecting a day route from each of the sub-areas. By doing this it ensures that the salesman is somewhere near all of his customers at least once a week. This means that when the unexpected request for a visit crops up, there will be a very good chance that the salesman will be in the area within the next day or so. In this way, the unexpected can be accommodated with minimum disruption to existing plans – again it also cuts down on costly special journeys.

By following the territory planning process outlined above, any salesman should be able to cut down on wasteful travelling and yet still be in a position to accommodate any sudden requests or complaints from customers.

As well as reducing costs, it provides the salesman with regular coverage of his territory and thereby provides more opportunity for customer contact. But what turns the opportunity into reality is the salesman's ability to obtain interviews.

Finally, whilst the A, B and C classification system suggested above is logical and tidy, there remains the question of whether existing and potential turnover should be the only determinant of call frequency.

Most salesmen would confess to a proclivity to call more frequently on those large customers who give them a friendly reception and less frequently on those who put business in their

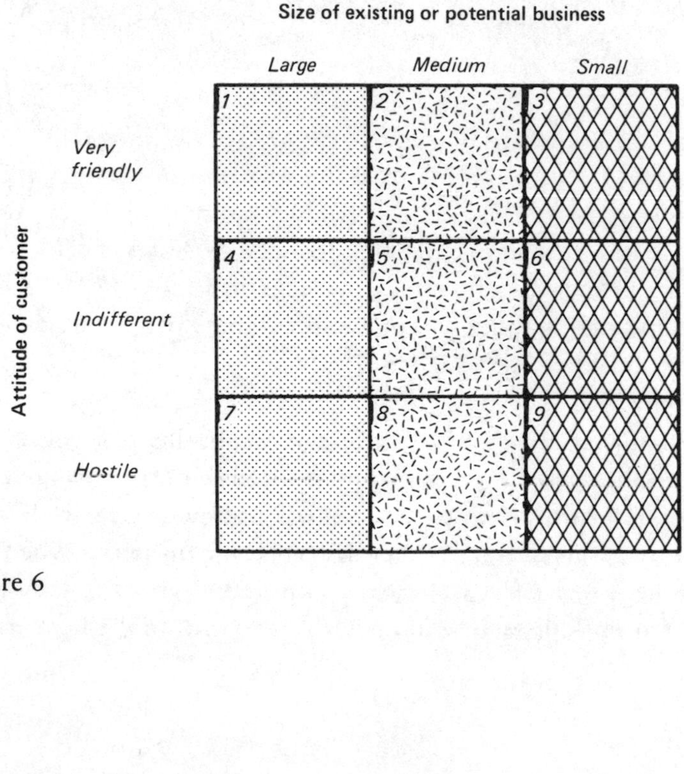

Figure 6

way. If we classify customers according to their friendliness to us as well as to their size, it is easy to see how a simple matrix can be developed to help us decide where our major effort should be directed.

From Figure 6 it can be seen that the boxes which offer the greatest potential for increased sales productivity are boxes 4 and 5, with boxes 1 and 2 receiving a 'maintenance' call rate. Boxes 7 and 8 should receive an 'alternative strategy' approach to establish whether the hostility can be overcome. If these alternative approaches fail, a lower call rate may be appropriate. Box 9 is the 'Don't bother' box, whilst boxes 3 and 6 will receive the minimum attention consistent with our goals.

None of this is meant to indicate definitive rules about call frequencies, which will always remain a matter of management judgment. Its sole purpose is to question our assumptions about call frequencies on existing and potential accounts to check that we are not using valuable time which could be more productively used in other directions.

Obtaining the interview

Obtaining interviews with regular customers is relatively easy and presents few problems for most salesmen. But what our territory plan shows up so clearly is the need to open new business with all those potential customers that we took into consideration. It means getting to know new buyers, new organizations, new decision-makers, and of one thing we can be sure – these people are all going to be very busy.

Not only will they have their normal day-to-day work to deal with, but also salesmen will be pressing to see them to lay claim to *even* more of their time. They will be familiar with being on the receiving end of numerous requests for appointments from sales-men. More often than not, they will have developed a 'screen' to protect them from this constant distracting bombardment. Gate-keepers, receptionists, secretaries or assistants will all have been instructed to keep speculative callers at bay.

The salesman, therefore, will have to put forward a good case if he is to stand a chance of meeting the buyer. It will not be enough to say, 'I am in the area and I would like to see you.'

Instead, the salesman must plan his approach in such a way that it will register with the buyer as being an interesting or attractive proposition.

What would this be? Well, in essence the message has to offer the buyer some benefit in *his* terms. It might be possible to offer him a possible solution to a problem he faces. It might be that your particular service could save him money. Perhaps your service will safeguard his interests in some way. Alternatively, your service might enable him to conduct his business more effectively.

Intelligent use of the basic customer research that we mentioned in the previous chapter will almost certainly provide important clues about how you might attract the buyer's interest. Never forget that a buyer will only see a salesman when he is convinced that there is a strong possibility that the salesman has something useful to offer.

Making the appointment

Most appointments are made by telephone, with the initiative for a time and date coming from the salesman. However, many people find that their success rate in gaining appointments is considerably increased if they precede their telephone call with a letter.

Such a letter ought to be short and punchy, designed in such a way that the buyer's interest will be aroused. It should also prepare him for the fact that you will be contacting him by telephone.

It is difficult to be prescriptive about the layout of this letter because by having a standard format much warmth and spontaneity, essential ingredients of good communication, might be lost.

However, by way of an example, here is an approach that ensures that the most important issues are covered.

1 Write down the name of the person to whom you are writing and make a note of his/her position in the company. Many people find that this helps them to focus on the recipient and to put themselves in the other person's shoes.
2 The first paragraph should be constructed to gain attention, get the reader thinking in the right context and should state the objective of the letter.
3 The second paragraph ought to state a problem which is high (or should be) on the reader's priority list. It will be important to phrase the problem in terms of how it makes impact on the reader.
4 Next will come a proposition which clearly shows how your service can meet the reader's needs or solve his problem in a cost-effective way.
5 It is often useful to substantiate the claim of the proposition by providing proof of how the service has helped other customers in similar circumstances to those of the reader.
6 Finally, the letter will close in a way which will make the reader want to hear more. For example, 'You will see from the cases I have quoted that the benefits from using our service(s) are both real and substantial. I have a proposition to discuss with you which I am convinced can produce similar savings at XYZ Ltd. I shall be telephoning next week to make an appointment to see you.'

A letter checklist is shown in Figure 7.

The initial letter to a prospective customer does not always have to originate from the salesman. Some companies spend considerable sums of money on advertising, mailshots and trade exhibitions, in order to get a regular stream of enquiries in the form of postage-paid cards, coupons and letters.

These enquiries should be passed to the appropriate salesman for him to follow up either by telephoning the enquirer, or more usually, by sending a letter and then telephoning.

In this way, there is a very high chance of converting enquiries into something more substantial. Unfortunately, many companies have yet to recognize the positive benefits of getting the salesmen to deal with enquiries. Instead, they take the unimaginative approach

A letter checklist

When you have drafted out your letter to the buyer, use this
list to check that it meets all these requirements

		YES	NO
1	Is the letter written from the viewpoint of the person to whom it is addressed?		
2	Does the opening secure favourable attention?		
3	Does it contain all the critical information necessary to achieve its purpose?		
4	Are the arguments in a logical order?		
5	Is the reader's problem really a high priority?		
6	Are the benefits listed those most likely to impress the reader?		
7	Are the proof statements adequate?		
8	Is the finish clear and positive?		
9	Is the general appearance good?		
10	Is it grammatically correct?		
11	Is it free of jargon?		
12	Is the punctuation correct?		
13	Are there any spelling errors?		
14	Is it free of trite, stilted or poorly chosen expressions?		
15	Is it easy to read?		
16	Can it be improved by shortening?		

Figure 7

of sending out bland letters and a brochure in response to enquiries. ('Thank you for your request for information about our latest brochure and information sheet. I trust that this will meet your requirements. Please don't hesitate to contact us again' . . . etc., etc.).

What a waste of good opportunities to make a sale!

Telephoning to make an appointment

To get the best out of the limited telephone contact time he will have with the prospective buyer, the salesman must be clear in his own mind what he wants to achieve from the call. Before he even dials the buyer's number, he should have gone through a carefully thought out set of preparatory steps.

Preparation

It is a good idea to allocate an hour or so on a regular basis just for making telephone appointments. It is easy to see why. Invariably some prospects will be unobtainable or out of their office for 'a few minutes'. When this happens the salesman can move to the next person on his list, rather than wait helplessly or keep ringing back to the same useless number.

1 Thus the first preparatory step is to consider the Territory Plan and from this list all the calls it will be necessary to make in order to arrange appointments.

Next, list all the telephone numbers, dialling codes and names of the contacts. It must be assumed that some contacts will not be available so, where it is possible, alternative contacts should be listed.

At this preparatory stage it is also useful to make notes about the contact's job title and the name of his/her secretary, if it is known.

2 After assembling all this relevant information about the 'targets', it is well worth the salesman spending a few minutes deciding

exactly what he wants to achieve from each call. He should make notes about the key questions or points that will need to be covered if he is to reach his objective.

It will be equally important, when it is relevant, to make notes about any issues, problems or queries that have arisen from previous calls. For example, if the sales records show that the buyer is very concerned about quality, then the salesman will be able to steer the conversation in this direction and improve his chances of arranging an appointment.

3 Decide how each conversation will be started. What words will be used? What tone of voice?

4 The salesman should have his diary open before him and have some very clear ideas about when he wants to meet the buyer. It must be the salesman's intention at all times to keep his travelling time to a minimum.

5 The telephoning is best done from a quiet office or room at home. If there is undue background noise, not only will the salesman have difficulty in hearing the customer, but also extraneous noise can be very disconcerting for the person on the other end of the line. This is particularly true when telephoning from home when a washing machine or TV can be plainly heard by the receiver, destroying any image of business efficiency that the salesman might be painstakingly trying to create.

Making the call

In making the call four possible outcomes are likely:

1 The line is busy, in which case the salesman ought not to waste any more time but instead try another customer.

2 The switchboard operator acts as a 'screen'.

3 The buyer's secretary acts as a 'screen'.

4 The switchboard puts the call immediately through to the buyer.

Dealing with the switchboard operator

Many operators do not ask questions, they make the connection almost automatically. However, there are some who have been asked to 'find out' more about callers. On asking to speak to Mr Buyer, this second type of operator will want to know the nature of the call.

The salesman's reply must be spontaneous and authoritative. For example:

'It's an important company matter.'

'It's about the Kuwait project.'

'It's about a letter I sent to him.'

The operator will find it difficult to press for further information without appearing to be rude, but if she does persist then the salesman runs the risk of becoming involved in detailed explanations. This could get distorted by the operator and perhaps lose much of its impact as it is passed on by her.

In these circumstances, the salesman would do better to try a different tactic and try to get away from the operator. He could say something like:

'I'm sorry but it's really too complex to ask you to pass on a message. Do you think it would be possible to put me through to Miss Williams, his secretary?'
(Ask for her by name or else use the opportunity to obtain the secretary's name).

Dealing with secretaries

At one time or another the salesman will have to deal with the buyer's secretary, who is likely to want to 'protect' her boss from unwelcome distractions.

Techniques for coping with secretaries can be similar to those given above for operators.

Better still, it might be worth trying a different approach, one which demonstrates that the salesman recognizes the secretary's importance. After all, it is worth remembering that she might well have access to Mr Buyer's diary. She might, in fact, be the best person to speak to with regard to obtaining an appointment.

The salesman could take the initiative:

'I wonder whether you can help me, Miss Williams? I want to see Mr Buyer about a very important business proposition which could save the company a lot of money.'

Note the use of the secretary's name. Having the secretary as an ally can dramatically improve the salesman's chances of arranging an interview.

Speaking to the prospect

Using the techniques mentioned above, the salesman will no doubt be connected to the person he wanted to speak to in the first place, Mr Buyer. What does he say now?

Hopefully, it will not be the first thing that comes into his head, because he should have a planned approach. Nor should it be some hackneyed expression like, 'I'm in your area next week and wonder if I could "pop" in to see you?' This almost invites a rejection, doesn't it?

The opening has to be carefully thought out.

1   The opening

It is good practice for the salesman to verify that he is indeed speaking to the right person. Some embarrassing misunderstandings have arisen at times when this simple start has been overlooked.

Another advantage is that it allows the salesman to use the buyer's name immediately.

'Hello. Is that Mr Buyer?'

'Yes.'

'Good afternoon, Mr Buyer. My name is . . . (here the salesman should introduce himself using both his first name and surname, also giving the name of his company). Can you spare me a minute?'

This approach is both courteous and reassuring to the buyer, in the sense that the call will not take up too much of his time. However, the pressure is now on the salesman to be brief.

The opening ought now to be followed by the lever.

2 *The connection*

This is a statement which does two things:
— it 'connects' the salesman with the buyer by reference to an earlier transaction, a mutual contact, a common interest or such like;
— it 'tunes' the buyer into the area of business upon which the salesman wishes to make impact.

As in a machine, making a connection generally sets something in motion, so the sales connection gets the interview moving into its business phase. Here are some examples of levers:

'Mr Buyer, have you received the letter I sent you about. . . ?'

'Mr Buyer, have you heard about our new. . . ?'

'Mr Buyer, your . . . (colleague, business associate, friend, etc. – use this person's name whenever possible) suggested that I contacted you about. . . .'

Note the use of Mr Buyer's name. There is evidence to show that prospective customers are flattered to hear their name from a stranger. It implies that the salesman has done his 'homework'.

Sometimes the salesman might not be able to think of an

appropriate connection. In this situation he could experiment with something like:

'Mr Buyer, did you read that article in the Journal about our company?'

If the reply is affirmative, then a connection is established. Should the reply be negative, well it doesn't matter too much; the salesman can say a few well chosen words about his company and move on to attempt to close.

3 The close

The whole objective of the call was to sell the idea that a visit would be worthwhile. In this form of telephone contact it is advisable to move on to the close as quickly as possible.

Here is an example of a close:

'I have noticed that you are continually advertising for experienced senior managers in the prestigious Sunday papers. The Management Placement Service we provide could, I believe, save you a considerable amount on your recruitment costs.

'It would take less than ten minutes to establish whether or not this is the case. Can we agree on a time when I could come to see you? How about next Tuesday afternoon? Or would Wednesday morning be more convenient?'

This type of quick close has several things to commend it:
— it provides quite a lot of information;
— it indicates benefits for the buyer;
— it is brief;
— it explains the nature of the business;
— it only asks for a short interview;
— it gives the salesman the initiative for fixing the appointment times;
— it closes, i.e., asks for the interview.
Note there is the implication that the salesman must have done

sufficient research to establish a good reason for arranging the appointment.

At this stage the buyer can only respond in one of two ways – accept the appointment or raise an objection.

Handling objections to appointments

While, in theory, there could be a host of possible objections, in practice objections against having a meeting seem to fall into two main types:

> 'I'm sorry, but I am too busy to see you' – sometimes substituted with or followed up by 'Can you send me some information?'
> or
> 'I do not need your service, thank you.'

Let us look at ways the salesman can respond to these objections.

The too busy objection

There are several ways of responding to this objection, but it should be noted that all of them start with the salesman acknowledging that he has heard the buyer say that he is busy. Never play down or dismiss a prospect's objection. To do so is to invite getting embroiled in an argument.

Here are some examples of ways to handle the objection:

> 'I do understand, Mr Buyer. There never seems to be enough hours in the day at this time of the year. Nevertheless, I am talking about the possibility of helping you to make substantial savings. We really ought to find some way to meet. Perhaps early one morning* or an evening might be more convenient?'

> 'I know, Mr Buyer, and that is another reason that we really

---

* The timing of appointments can be critical. This is considered in more detail later.

ought to meet, because not only will our Management Placement Service will save your company money, it will also cut down the demands on your time.'

'I know, Mr Buyer. But in my experience, if you want a job done well or to get results you have to go to the busy people. That is why it is so important that I see you . . . and don't forget, we could be talking about considerable savings. . . .'

Should none of these work then the salesman can always suggest that he calls back in two or three weeks time when the buyer might be less busy. An alternative is to suggest that he will take a chance and call in at the company next time he is passing.

Few prospects will refuse such requests because in their eyes there is no risk to them, they are still in 'control'. However, if the salesman persistently follows up in the way he has promised, he will almost certainly eventually get his appointment.

The request for further information

Again, it is possible to have several replies at one's disposal. Here are some examples:

'I would be delighted to send you further information Mr Buyer, but in our experience every client company has different requirements. It would only take a few minutes of your time to establish exactly how we could give you best value.'

'We do in fact have a lot of information, Mr Buyer. I'll bring it with me. It will take only a few minutes to explain the relevant points and that will save you time ploughing through some less important items.'

'Mr Buyer, I would be doing you a disservice if I sent you the wrong information just because I didn't know one or two important facts about your situation. It will only take a few minutes. . . .'

The aim of all these counters to the request for further information is to demonstrate that the prospect will only get the full, accurate facts through a face-to-face meeting.

An added benefit is the implication that it will be easier for the buyer to assimilate the information if the salesman is there to explain.

Don't need the service objection

The problem for the salesman is to establish as quickly as possible whether or not this is a true statement or is just being used as an excuse to fob him off.

Thus the salesman must gently but politely probe to seek more information. He might try the following type of approach:

'I'm sorry to hear that Mr Buyer. Does that mean your recruitment programme has finished?'

'I'm sorry to hear that Mr Buyer. But perhaps you could help me, because we are always looking for ways to improve our Management Placement Service. How would a company like yours plan to handle senior recruitment in the coming year?'

There is always a possibility that the objection might be genuine but the earlier research should be directing the salesman to those companies where there is a need for the service.

A variation on this type of objection is:

'We already have someone providing this service.'

Again the salesman needs to get more information and yet try for an appointment. He could try this approach:

'Thank you for being so frank with me Mr Buyer. Could you tell me who it is?'

(Generally the buyer will divulge who supplies the service and the salesman continues thus):

'They are a very reputable organization, Mr Buyer. But you might care to know that we are the fastest growing company in this field. That does suggest that we are very competitive, doesn't it, Mr Buyer? It could pay you to have more information about competing services and charges. Can we meet?'

The main point to note here is that the successful salesman never 'knocks' the opposition. To be disparaging about a competitor is to infer that the buyer's judgement is faulty.

Another point is that a new lever is introduced, i.e. the usefulness of having more information, before attempting the close.

Confirming the appointment

As soon as the buyer agrees to a meeting on a particular day, the salesman ought to confirm things immediately.

'Thank you, Mr Buyer. I look forward to meeting you on . . . (date) at . . . (time).'

This is a courteous conclusion to a businesslike exchange and ensures that there are no misunderstandings.

If the arrangements are for a first appointment with either a large company or an important buyer, then it is excellent practice to confirm the appointment by letter.

Timing of appointments

When suggesting a date and time for an appointment, the salesman is attempting to control his daily timetable and thereby keep his unproductive travelling to a minimum.

However, even though the buyer wants to see him, the salesman is still competing with many others for the buyer's time. It is, therefore, good tactics to suggest slightly unusual times for appointments because this can increase the chances of seeing the buyer on the day most convenient to the salesman.

There are a number of possibilities.

Early in the day

With many companies working flexi-hours, a surprisingly large number of people choose to start work early. Thus between the hours of 8.00 am and 9.30 am (when the morning post is usually delivered and the telephone gets busy) many prospective buyers will be available; but what is even more important, they will not be under as much pressure as they will undoubtedly be later in the day.

Late in the day

Similar advantages can be found if the salesman aims for appointments between 4.30 pm and, with some executives still being available, as late as 7.00 pm.

An added advantage for the salesman getting appointments early or late in the day is that he will be able to increase the number of calls he makes.

Monday mornings and Friday afternoons

A myth is perpetuated that nobody wants to see salesmen at these times. It is claimed to be impossible to fix appointments.

Maybe lazy salesmen, who in effect prefer to work a four-day week, will fight shy of making appointments on Monday mornings or Friday afternoons. But think of the scope this leaves for their other more ambitious contemporaries.

Lunchtimes

Although some prospects will be unobtainable between 12.00 and

2.30 pm, not all of them will be absent at the same time. In reality, perhaps only a half-hour, round about 1.00–1.30 pm, is 'dead' time.

For the remaining period it is often possible to see a prospect. And don't forget that many executives might, instead of going to lunch, have a snack in their office.

Nightshift

It is possible that a key member of the D.M.U. is on the night shift at his company. Such a prospect will rarely see a salesman in the normal run of events and so his receptivity for a meeting will be very high.

From the salesman's point of view, competition is zero.

Unusual times

Salesmen tend to fall into a pattern of fixing appointments on the hour or at half past. Since the telephone call making the appointment has talked of 'taking ten minutes of your time', why not ask for appointments at unusual times such as 9.50 am or 3.20 pm?

This means that the prospect might well try to 'squeeze' in an extra meeting, and if it overruns, take comfort from the fact that it is some other, less imaginative salesman left waiting outside.

The key to timing appointments is to find out what best suits the contacts. There is no reason why the salesman should not ask his customers which day of the week is most convenient for them and what time of the day is best.

By keeping records of this information and knowing a broad range of acceptable visiting times, the salesman can really get down to planning a good day's work.

Running late

With the best will in the world, sometimes events will happen which cause the salesman's day plan to break down. A meeting overruns here, a delay there, a traffic jam between companies.

Generally speaking, underrunning on time does not present the salesman with problems. He can always find some productive use for the time he has 'saved'.

However, running late is a much more serious matter because it is not just the salesman who is affected, it is all the prospects he hopes to see for the rest of the day.

It will be essential for the salesman to telephone ahead to warn his contacts that his schedule is running late. Sometimes people will be very accommodating and put back their appointments.

A polite request at the client company will invariably put a telephone at his disposal and the salesman can then 'phone ahead to explain his problem to the next buyer. This is important for two reasons:

1 The salesman can relax knowing that his next contact knows what is happening.
2 Public telephones that work can never be found when they are needed, thus the salesman can cause himself even more tension and anxiety as he tries to make up lost time on the road.

More usually, to change arrangements at short notice will inconvenience the prospects. In these circumstances it might be better to rearrange the next appointment and then get back on schedule with the others.

Good preparation

The key lesson from this chapter about reaching the customers is that *good preparation is essential.*

Without the necessary preparation the salesman cannot make a sensible territory plan; he will not be able to plan economical daily routes, approach the right customers or arrange appointments.

As we have seen, the amount of planning and forethought is not excessive, yet it is a measure of the difference between the successful salesman and his mediocre counterpart.

Application questions

1 On what basis do you plan your call schedules? What led you to use this approach? Can you think of any ways in which you can improve your call planning?

2 How successful are you in obtaining interviews with new prospects? What do you find to be the most effective approach? What other approaches might be helpful for you to add to your 'repertoire'?

3 In your particular business, do you use letters as levers to obtain interviews? What other levers do you use? What new levers could you use to advantage?

4 What do you think should be the role of your head office when they receive customer enquiries? Should they be dealt with by head office? Should they be passed directly to you? Should there be some compromise between these two approaches? (How would it operate?)

5 Some ideas about telephone approaches are discussed in this chapter. Can you identify any ways to improve on these suggestions?

6 In your particular business, what are the most suitable times for arranging appointments? Have you ever deliberately tried fixing an appointment for an 'unusual' time? What happened?

7 In this chapter some ideas were put forward for dealing with receptionists and secretaries. Can you suggest any ways to improve upon the methods suggested?

Exercises

Exercise 2.1: *A typical day*

Imagine that you have just been discussing with a group of other salesmen all the activities a salesman has to fit into a typical day. Probably not all of these activities will apply to your particular job, but make a note of those that do.

Using the accompanying worksheet, draw a 'pie' chart for a typical day, making each 'slice of the pie' roughly proportioned to the time spent on each activity.

Study the completed pie chart and ask yourself which of the activities gives you most satisfaction. Against this, write (1) in the outer ring. Then identify the second most satisfying activity and denote this with (2) in the outer ring and so on until all activities are covered.

Please note that there does not necessarily have to be any correlation between the size of the pie chart slices and the satisfaction derived from that activity.

Having completed the pie chart and added all the satisfaction 'scores' please answer these questions.

1 In what practical ways could you reduce those areas of non-productive time?
2 In which area(s) could this saved time best be used?
3 How would your revised day affect your levels of satisfaction, i.e. will you be spending more time on those activities that give you high satisfaction (low scores) or not?
4 What could you or your company do to improve the level of satisfaction in those activities which are necessary but demotivating, i.e. received a high score on the worksheet?

Worksheet

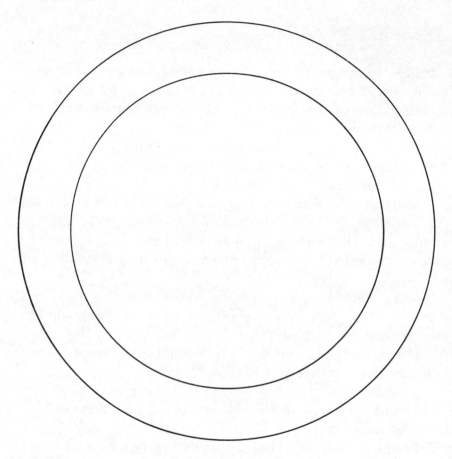

Figure 8

Exercise 2.2:　Territory planning

Doubtless in Exercise 2.1 'travelling time' featured somewhere in the 'areas of non-productive time to reduce' section. One way to make impact on travelling time is to re-appraise the way you schedule your visits to customers. Often revised forms of route planning can lead to considerable savings.

Let us try out the ideas put forward in Chapter 2.

Step 1

Go through your customer records and, using your experience of your particular business, classify each customer into one of the following categories:

High actual (or potential) sales value i.e. above £ ....

Medium ....

Low .... i.e. below £ ....

You decide which values to put in the £ ....spaces

As a rough guideline only something like 15 per cent of your customers ought to fall into your high sales category, so choose the sales level figure with this in mind. Similarly, something like 25 per cent to 30 per cent of your customers ought to feature in the low sales category. The reason for choosing these seemingly arbitrary figures can best be explained by referring to the graph below.

Whenever sales value versus customer ranking is plotted out in graphical form, this typical shape always seems to be the result. Knowing this it becomes possible to predict that the top 15 per cent to 20 per cent of the customer portfolio will be extremely valuable, accumulatively accounting for something like 75 per cent of the sales revenue.

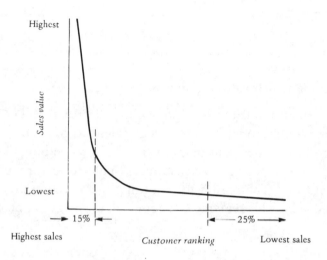

In comparison, the bottom 25 per cent to 30 per cent will collectively contribute only a relatively small sales revenue.

Clearly the difference between customers in the top bracket and those in the bottom needs to be taken into account in terms of how the salesman spends his most limited resource – *time* i.e. visiting and maintaining contact. And what about customers in the middle range, how should they be treated? But for now, just complete your classification of customers in the way described above.

Step 2

Obtain a large scale map of your territory and if possible, mount it on a board and cover it with clear plastic.

Step 3

Using different coloured marker pins to represent your three categories of customers (high, medium and low sales), identify every customer location on your map with a pin. This pictorial representation of your territory will be at the heart of your planning process, but for now we will leave it to consider another issue.

Step 4

It will now be important to estimate the total time you will have at your disposal to 'work' your territory. To do this you might need to refer back to Exercise 2.1 to ensure that you incorporate any new ideas from there into your calculations.

1   How many working days will be available in the coming year? (remember to take holidays, etc. into account)   _ _ _ _ _ _ _ _ _

2   How many days are lost to attending necessary meetings or other unavoidable non-sales activities?   _ _ _ _ _ _ _ _ _

3   Subtract 2 from 1 to give the number of selling days available.   _ _ _ _ _ _ _ _ _

4   How many calls are possible each day?   _ _ _ _ _ _ _ _ _

5   Total number of calls available in the year is 3 multiplied by 4.   _ _ _ _ _ _ _ _ _

Step 5

Work out a call strategy for dealing with your different categories of customers. For example, the top bracket high sales value customers might merit a high number of service calls on a regular basis, whereas the bottom category might only require an occasional visit, most contact being by letter or telephone. The middle category might be something else again.

Note: Exercise 2.3 will probably be helpful to you at this stage. (This is the only part of your study programme where you are invited to leave an exercise before completion to move to another.)

Step 6

Using your call strategy from Step 5, try to balance the following sum:

Number of top bracket customers × their call frequency =
Number of medium bracket customers × their call frequency =
Number of bottom bracket customers × their call frequency =

Total: _____

Note: The *total* should be the figure arived at in Step 4, the total number of calls available.

Should the above sum not 'add up', then call frequencies will have to be revised accordingly. If call frequencies are embarrassingly high and there is a surplus of calls available, then clearly more time will need to be invested in prospecting and building up a bigger customer portfolio.

Step 7

Using the ideas from Chapter 2, divide your territory into five sub-areas (one for each day of the week), each of a similar workload in terms of calls required. Within each sub-area, work out a series of daily routes which have approximately the same sales potential and keep travel to a minimum.

Step 8

Complete your territory plan by devising a schedule of customer visits aimed at maximizing contact and minimizing travel. For example:

Week 1: Day 1   Sub-area 1   Route 1
          Day 2   Sub-area 2   Route 1
          Day 3   Sub-area 3   Route 1
          Day 4   Sub-area 4   Route 1
          Day 5   Sub-area 5   Route 1

Week 2: Day 1   Sub-area 1   Route 2
          Day 2   Sub-area 2   Route 2
          Day 3   Sub-area 3   Route 2
          Day 4   Sub-area 4   Route 2
          Day 5   Sub-area 5   Route 2

To avoid being in the same sub-area on the same day each week, either switch sub-areas in the planning sequence or organize the territory using only four sub-areas, which in effect means that one sub-area is visited twice in any one week, eg:

Week 1: Day 1   Sub area 1   Route 1
          Day 2   Sub-area 2   Route 1
          Day 3   Sub-area 3   Route 1
          Day 4   Sub-area 4   Route 1
          Day 5   Sub-area 1   Route 2

Week 2: Day 1   Sub-area 2   Route 2
          Day 2   Sub-area 3   Route 2
          Day 3   Sub-area 4   Route 2
          Day 4   Sub-area 1   Route 3
          Day 5   Sub-area 2   Route 3

Exercise 2.3: *Customer call strategies*

In Exercise 2.2 we saw how important it was to have a customer call strategy if one is to arrive at a sensible territory plan. This exercise is intended to stimulate some new ways of looking at call strategies and builds on the idea of customer classification developed in Exercise 2.2. Remember, there were three groups of customers:

High actual or potential sales
Medium actual or potential sales
Low actual or potential sales

These groupings are based on a quantitative assessment of the customers.

However, we know from experience that our dealings with customers are heavily influenced by the ease with which we can relate to them. For example, some are friendly and we feel relaxed in our dealings with them. Others are hostile, which makes us tense and puts us on our guard. There are others still who could be said to be indifferent, perhaps tending to be formal and polite. We always feel with these customers that if only we could get behind the facade, get closer to them, we could probably help them much more than when we are held at arm's length.

The quality of our relationship with each customer clearly has an effect on the amount of business we can expect to develop. It is possible to combine the customer classification ideas with the more subjective thinking about relationships in the matrix on page 83.

Using the matrix work out what, in your opinion, ought to be the most successful call strategy to employ for each of the nine groups (boxes) of customers.

Note: For the purposes of this exercise, any new customers, where the relationship is hardly established, should be 'lumped' with the indifferent ones.

After you have made notes about your call strategies, check them against the suggestions made in Chapter 2. If they are not in broad agreement, read through that particular section again.

Size of existing or potential business

	High actual or potential sales	Medium actual or potential sales	Low actual or potential sales
Very friendly	1	2	3
Indifferent	4	5	6
Hostile	7	8	9

Attitude of customer

Exercise 2.4: *Writing a sales letter*

Many salesmen find that their ability to secure an interview over the telephone is increased if they precede their call with a letter. However, writing a sales letter is a skill which has to be learned. There may be a fortunate few who are 'naturals' when it comes to writing sales letters, but most of us are not. Take the example of the following letter. The writer, Mr G. H. Bennett is not an uneducated man and he is a very experienced bank manager. What do you think of his 'sales letter'?

INTERNATIONAL BANK LIMITED

Commercial Street   Our Ref: GHB/jf
Ourtown
West Midlands
OT2 2LG

The Managing Director   27 February 1988
Acme Engineering Co Ltd
Britannia Industrial Estate
Ourtown
West Midlands

Dear Sir

I have recently taken over the management of the Ourtown Branch of the International Bank and am endeavouring to make contact with as many representatives of local businesses as possible.

I am not of course in possession of full details of your Company but feel sure there will be many areas in which we can be of assistance.

Many companies from time to time require finance and in addition to the normal facilities in this respect the bank's Business Development Loan Scheme provides assistance well suited for expansion plans which involve the purchase/extension of premises and/or the provision of new machinery. It may be of course that finance could be required, geared towards working capital and you may find details of the bank's factoring operations including invoice discounting of interest in this respect.

We do, of course, through our subsidiary, International Data Services, offer a full payroll service with the many benefits including cost savings this represents, together with a full accounting service and other ancillary computer based services.

Commercial insurance too is available through International Insurance Services Limited, one of the largest broking companies in the country and able therefore to bring to bear the full resources of the bank to offer the best all round package to fulfil all your company's insurance needs from vehicle cover to pension plans.

I have taken the opportunity of enclosing leaflets giving more details of the services I have mentioned, together with a further selection of material that gives an indication of the very wide financial package the bank can offer.

It would I am sure be of mutual benefit if we can meet and discuss ways in which we could assist and to this end I await your response when we may make the necessary arrangements.

Yours faithfully

G. H. Bennett
Manager

Step 1

Write down all the points about this letter where you think improvements could be made.

Step 2

Compare your critique of the letter with the suggestions put forward in the Answer Section on page 223.

Step 3

Observing all the 'rules' for improvement to a sales letter developed in Steps 1 and 2, write a sales letter to a potential customer of yours.

Note: It is intended that you should be prepared to send the final version of your letter to an *actual* customer.

Step 4

After posting the letter and allowing for delivery and reading time, telephone the customer with a view to arranging an appointment.

Exercise 2.5:   Securing an appointment

This exercise is designed to help you to prepare for making appointments over the telephone and to become more aware of the factors that contribute to developing a successful telephone technique to secure appointments.

Brief

Imagine that you are a representative of Spick and Span Ltd, a young expanding firm of office cleaning contractors; your manager has given you a lead to follow up at Rational Pension Assurance Ltd. The contact is a Neil Henderson, the Management Services Manager, who is based at R.P.A.'s administrative headquarters which occupies twelve floors of a large office block in a city centre.

Your manager's exact words were: 'I met their Sales Director at that conference last week. I understand this chap Henderson is fed up with the level of service he is getting from their current cleaning contractor. It shouldn't be too difficult to get an appointment and try to win a new contract for us.

You decide to telephone Henderson to secure an appointment. It is Monday.

Step 1

Prepare a plan for this call using the suggestions outlined in Chapter 2 i.e. consider:

1   The opening
2   The lever
3   The close
4   Handling objections
5   Confirming the appointment

Compare your plan with the suggested one given on page 225. If there is any substantial variation of principle, rather than the words used, then it will probably be helpful for you to read the section on this topic in Chapter 2.

Step 2

When you ring through to the company, Henderson is not available and you have to speak to his secretary. Write the way you would handle this situation. Check your answer on page 226.

Step 3

The secretary comes up with these 'blocks'. Write down how you would reply to them.

1   'Mr Henderson is tied up this week because he is preparing to be away on holiday for three weeks from next Monday and is busy arranging for others to cover for him.'
2   'He only sees representatives on Thursday and Friday afternoons and is fully tied up at these times.'
3   'Let me take a message.'

Check your answer with the suggestions given on page 226.

Step 4

You are connected to Mr Henderson and he raises these objections at various times during the interview:

1   'Our current contractors say they will improve.'
2   'I get fed up with being pestered by salesmen.'
3   'I don't know much about your company.'
4   'I'm really busy, I don't think I can find time to meet you for a
     few weeks.'

Write down how you would respond to them and then check your replies with those given on page 227.

3

Opening the Sales Interview

Overview

The opening moments of a sales interview are of the utmost importance because in that time the first impressions that are formed in the buyer's mind can dictate how the interview proceeds.

The salesman therefore has to plan how to handle the interview effectively and get it off to a good start. He will set clear objectives for each call and from these develop action plans.

He will pay particular attention to organizing his presentation into a logical sequence and using the most appropriate behaviour to achieve his call objectives. Whenever appropriate he will prepare supporting material or visual aids to underpin or illuminate the information he wishes to convey to the buyer.

He also needs to plan the best way to open the sales interview. The technique he chooses and the actual choice of opening words will be critical to the subsequent success of the meeting.

In attempting to gain the attention of the buyer, arouse his interest and build his confidence, the salesman must also pay attention to his own well-being. He must arrive early for appointments and avoid unnecessary self-imposed stresses.

The salesman must constantly watch his personal appearance and behaviour to ensure that he does nothing to diminish the customer's confidence.

However, appearance isn't the only 'spoiler': drinking, time-wasting and not paying due attention to the buyer and his needs can all play their part in prejudicing the chances of success in the sales meeting.

Opening the sales interview

The reader who adapts to his situation the key messages outlined in Chapter 2 will significantly improve his capability to reach customers and gain interviews.

However, the most testing and, in many ways, the most exciting part of the selling process is now about to begin – the face-to-face meeting.

All of us have at one time or another been a customer, and so we know from personal experience that the first impression made by the salesman can have a disproportionate impact on us. If the salesman looks and acts 'the part', treats us with respect, puts us at ease and talks about our needs, then he will almost certainly win our attention.

Conversely, the salesman who is sloppy, both in appearance and in behaviour, will have to work very hard to overcome the instinctive prejudices built up in those first, vital minutes of contact.

The opening phase of the sales interview is therefore too important to be left to chance and that is why successful salesmen invest a lot of time and imagination in their preparation.

Pre-call planning

The need for information about the buyer, his company, his company's products or services, standing in the marketplace, organizational problems and so on, have already been stressed in the foregoing chapters.

In addition to this customer research, other equally important preparation will be required.

The call objectives

The salesman must be clear in his mind about the purpose of the call. Without clear objectives it will be impossible to make any sensible preparations.

Remember at this stage that it isn't always appropriate to make the initial objective one of closing the sale. There might be many other types of call objectives, depending upon the nature of the salesman's relationship with the buyer, the buy phase of the transaction and level of contact with members of the D.M.U. Here are some examples of other, equally valid call objectives:

— to establish who are the key executives who influence the buying process;
— to present a quotation;
— to provide information about new developments incorporated in our services;
— to obtain an introduction to the managing director;
— to obtain an agreement to give a demonstration/presentation to the relevant people in the client company;
— to handle a complaint;
— to negotiate a long-term contract.
  The list is almost endless.

The objectives ought to be sufficiently specific so that the salesman will be able to measure whether or not he has achieved them by the end of the sales call. All those listed above meet this criterion.

Sometimes it is not so easy to establish measurable call objectives, for example where it is intended 'to maintain goodwill'. However, by focusing on what goodwill could mean in client terms, it should be possible to arrive at a set of secondary objectives such as:

— to establish that the service is meeting customer expectations;
— to inform the buyer about new technology changes in the market-place, etc;
— to obtain a date for a future meeting;
— to identify information needs at the client company;
— to find out about competitor activity in the particular service field;

All of these are just as measurable as those above.

Having established call objectives, the salesman must now apply himself to deciding the best way to achieve them.

Action planning

The planning will fall into five parts:

1 Working out a sequence of logical steps that will need to be covered in order to reach the objective.
2 Calculating what behaviours are most likely to be required to achieve the objectives.
3 Deciding what sort of aids or supporting material would genuinely help to achieve the call objective.
4 If there is a possibility of having any choice, deciding the most appropriate venue for the meeting.
5 Putting together an opening statement or question which will get the interview off to a good start.

Let us look at each of these in more detail.

1   A logical sequence

The salesman must plan (and remember his plan) for achieving the call objective. So before the interview he will make a list of all the points he wishes to cover.

The next step will be to rewrite these in the sequence that makes the most logical and easy-to-follow presentation.

Then he must decide how each point will be covered systematically. Invariably, this will mean marshalling a number of facts, features and benefits.

Many salesmen find that they can plan their presentation, but then have great difficulty remembering the sequence once they are face-to-face with the buyer and perhaps under some stress. The successful salesman must therefore develop techniques to guard against such lapses of memory.

Although the preparation is probably in the form of a list, it is unlikely to be appropriate to keep referring to it while in conversation with the buyer. Such behaviour is unlikely to inspire confidence. Any memory aids must therefore be less intrusive than checklists, scripts or prompts and not interfere with the flow of the conversation.

Some salesmen use mnemonics to help them remember their planned sequence. By making a word from initial letters on their list or a rhyme from key points, it is possible to get instant recall. A useful mnemonic for a sales situation is A.B.C.* – *Attention, Benefits, Close.* Indeed, because of its usefulness, this mnemonic provides the framework for the rest of this textbook.

Clearly the opening of the sales interview is all about gaining the buyer's *attention*, then as the interview progresses the *benefits* of the service have to be put convincingly to the buyer. Finally, after it has been shown how the service will meet the customer's needs, the salesman will *close* the interview and meet his objectives. Mnemonics like A.B.C. are therefore most helpful.

Probably most of us can still recall from our schooldays the colours of the rainbow by remembering that 'Richard of York gave *battle in vain*', i.e., red, orange, yellow, green, blue, indigo, violet.

There are many other examples, but for those who like to invent their own mnemonics it is claimed that unusual, absurd or even vulgar words or phrases are better memory joggers than run-of-the-mill language.

Some salesmen find that they can remember their plan sequence by inventing a visual picture. The picture itself does not have to be logical. For example, if someone had five steps to cover he might recall them as a hand with spread fingers and on each one written a key word.

Alternatively, it is possible to visualize the key words stacked like bricks upon each other, or in some other distinctive pattern.

We know of one salesman, who happened to be a keen musician. He visualized his sales sequence as notes of music on a musical score.

* This technique was developed by Alfred Tack of the Tack Organisation and we are grateful to him for his permission to use it.

Sometimes a key sentence will provide the necessary reminder. In fact some companies invent such sentences to help the salesman describe the idea, product or service and also provide the benefit. For example:

'Phyllosan fortifies the over forties.'

'Cranfield School of Management: good in theory, great in practice.'

These, then, are some techniques that a salesman can use to remember his presentation sequence. There are probably many others. As they become experienced, most salesmen develop their own systems.

2   Behaviour

Just as the content of the sales call has to be planned in order to achieve the objective, so must some consideration be given to the salesman's behaviour or inter-action with the buyer. If this is inappropriate it can cause unnecessary barriers to the transaction.

What sort of behaviours need to be considered? Well, think of the opening to the meeting. The salesman will wish to establish a good rapport with the buyer as quickly as possible. A warm, friendly smile and a firm handshake while keeping eye contact can succeed in creating a favourable impression immediately. In fact, keeping good eye contact throughout the meeting is helpful in establishing trust and rapport. This doesn't mean that the meeting becomes a 'staring match'. If it feels like that, then the eye contact is being overdone.

The salesman who shows enthusiasm for his service and concern for the buyer's needs is always better received than his less enthusiastic counterpart.

In a survey we did for a company a little while ago, we actually asked buyers how they reacted to the company's salesmen. We were not altogether surprised to find that in our sample of buyers, over half of them said that the salesmen *talked too much* and didn't listen to their problems.

The salesman therefore in his preparation will have to plan to listen more carefully. But this doesn't mean just sitting quietly 'soaking up' all that is said. It is important to let the buyer know that he has been heard.

Instead of just nodding whenever the buyer speaks, the salesman should from time to time summarize what the buyer has been saying AND ADD his interpretation of how the buyer felt (or feels) about the situation.

This might sound difficult at first, but with practice it comes automatically. Here is an example:

'You seem to be saying that all those problems were caused because you did not have a sufficiently large design department. You must have felt very frustrated at the time Mr Buyer.'

This form of 'active listening', as it is called, does three things:

1   It demonstrates that the salesman is really listening.
2   It enables the salesman to check that he understands what has been said.
3   By connecting the buyer's feelings with the event under discussion the salesman is showing empathy with the buyer, i.e., showing that he can imagine how it must feel to be in the buyer's shoes.

Research has shown* that successful salesmen are those who have high empathy with their customers. What other behaviour planning might be considered?

We all have mannerisms of one sort or another and sometimes these can adversely affect the outcome of our sales interviews. For example, some salesmen interrupt when the other person is

* Myers and Greenburg, 'What Makes a Good Salesman?' in *Harvard Business Review*, Issue 4, 1964.

speaking; some salesmen finish off the sentence for the buyer (this is more likely to happen if the buyer talks slowly); and so on.

There are in addition many other personal mannerisms too numerous to mention. If we are conscious of having any such mannerisms, or if a trusted colleague has hinted that we have one, then we really ought to try to eradicate it.

Over familiarity is also a problem for some salesmen. They misinterpret a friendly approach on the part of the buyer as something more significant than it was intended to be.

The salesman should remain polite and courteous at all times.

Part of our behaviour is non-verbal, the so-called body language. The way we sit and stand can tell an onlooker much about us. For example, while we might tell the buyer we are really interested in hearing about the history of his company, unknown to us our facial expression and posture are proclaiming how bored we really are.

Therefore the salesman should always try to sit or stand in a conventional pose and be relaxed. Whenever possible try to sit adjacent to the buyer and try not to be forced to conduct business across a large desk. The actual distance between two people can inhibit their interaction and communication.

3 Supporting material and visual aids

If you believe the service you supply is valuable, then any visual aid or supporting materials should be seen as equally important and must be prepared with great care.

Support material must be:
- relevant;
- well presented;
- complete;
- in good order;
- checked regularly and up-dated when necessary.

Sales literature and sales aids should always be kept in a brief case or special folder in a pre-planned order. This will enable the salesman to extract the appropriate leaflet or picture without taking his attention away from the buyer.

No salesman should ever be in the position where he has to say:

'I'm sorry that this doesn't work too well, but it's only a demonstration model – the actual one you will receive will be better than this.'

or

'I'm sorry that this brochure is a bit dog-eared, they seem to be in short supply at the moment.'

Apologies like this indicate inefficiency on someone's part, and it would probably be better to put off such a demonstration until you have the right model or not to show a brochure at all, rather than produce a scruffy document out of your briefcase.

It is well-known that if we only hear a message, we are less likely to remember it than if we hear it and are given a visual reinforcement of the message at the same time. In fact, as a general rule, the more senses that can be appealed to at the same time, then the more the receiver of the information is likely to remember it. Thus seeing and hearing is better than just hearing alone. Seeing, hearing and touching or handling is better still, and if taste and smell can be incorporated also, when appropriate, the buyer will be more likely to remember the main points the salesman is trying to communicate.

It is this appeal to additional senses that makes visual aids so valuable. However, a picture on its own is not always enough. There is a danger that the viewer will misinterpret it or make incorrect assumptions about his own level of knowledge. Just think about when we read a car repair manual. Every job sounds so simple and the diagrams are so explicit. Then we lift the bonnet of the car to start the job . . . !!!

So the salesman must use his visual aids to reinforce what he tells the customer and make sure that he gives any necessary additional information to define accurately what is in the picture.

Many companies now prepare tape-slide, film-strip or videotape presentations for their salesmen to use. In many respects moving visual aids are more dramatic and memorable than stills, but even so they are not substitutes for the salesman. He will still have to work to connect the pictures to the buyer's situation and draw attention to the pertinent parts of the presentation.

Company brochures can be useful visual aids, but sometimes they are overstocked with technical information and data. This is not meant as a criticism of the brochure, since it is designed to stand alone and provide such information.

However, in order to simplify the visual message, the salesman can, if necessary, eliminate some of the technical clutter. The relevant pictures can be resequenced in a plastic leafed, visual aids folder, perhaps with additional photographs added to make a more logical presentation.

With such a folder at his disposal, the salesman can control the nature and the depth of technical information that is given to his contacts.

Demonstrations Perhaps the ultimate visual aid is the demonstration. Of course, with many services, practical demonstrations are not possible. With others, however, such as an office supplies service, design consultancy, or video service and so on, it is often useful to demonstrate examples of previous work. Like everything else, it too has to be planned if it is to be successful.

Generally speaking demonstrations are only used when either
— the salesman cannot adequately explain from diagrams and pictures how the service actually works; or
— the salesman has to prove to the customer that the service can achieve the results claimed for it.

In the initial planning of the demonstration a number of points need to be considered:
— what will be a successful end result?
— who will be attending? (Both the number and their job titles.)
— where will the demonstration take place?
— when?
— what equipment, literature, samples, etc., will be required?
— who is best suited to give the demonstration, i.e., are other people likely to be involved?

Having answered these questions and prepared accordingly, just before the demonstration takes place it will be important to check that any visual aids are in good working order and that colleagues who are involved are well briefed.

During the actual demonstration always explain to the customer what he is going to see. It also helps to break the demonstration sequence into a number of separate parts. This makes it so much easier for the observer to follow.

Always allow enough time for people to ask questions and, if it is safe enough for them to do so, let the customer actually handle the equipment.

Obviously, if the operation requires a lot of skill or some special knack, then it will be unwise to let the customer use the equipment. Even so, in these circumstances it is still generally possible to let him push a button or handle a component as it comes out of the machine. Remember what was said earlier about appealing to as many of the senses as possible?

There is another good reason for not allowing the customer to use the equipment if special skills are needed. Once he finds it difficult to use, it might be hard convincing him that his staff would be able to handle it if he bought the equipment.

At the end of the demonstration, summarize what the customer has just seen and use the opportunity to re-emphasize the special features and benefits of your particular service.

It is often a good idea to find an excuse to leave the customer alone for a short while so that he can talk about the demonstration in private.

Lastly, at the end of the demonstration remember to thank everyone who was involved.

4 Choice of venue for the meeting

The salesman needs the buyer's undivided attention at the meeting. Therefore, in his pre-call planning, he must give some thought to the surroundings in which the meeting will take place.

If he knows or suspects the buyer is located in a noisy or distracting area, for example, somewhere where the telephone is

continually ringing, the salesman might suggest an alternative
meeting place – perhaps a local hotel, over lunch.

The choice of venue is not always the salesman's prerogative.
Nevertheless, should he find himself trying to conduct a conversation in inappropriate surroundings, it is only sensible to ask if the
meeting could continue in a quieter area or somewhere where
confidential information will not be overheard.

5 Planning the opening statement

As we have said before, the first half minute or so of any meeting is
critical. It is in that time that the buyer will make up his mind
whether or not it is going to be worth listening to the salesman. He
will have made a rapid assessment of the salesman's overall
appearance in that time and will now want to hear something that
will interest him and hold his attention.

Therefore the salesman should aim to explain the purpose of his
visit at a very early stage.

Pleasantries There will be a natural inclination to exchange
pleasantries at the beginning of the conversation. Indeed, not to do
so could be construed as the height of discourtesy by some buyers.
However, there is a danger that this can be overdone. It is all very
well to talk about the weather, holidays, illness in the family, the
latest news, the Test Match score and so on, but this isn't going to
get the business done.

As a general rule keep pleasantries to a minimum, especially at
first meetings. Later, as relationships develop, it might become
more appropriate to spend a little longer on this phase of the
conversation.

Another general rule is for the salesman not to talk about himself
but the buyer. For example, if it is felt that talking about holidays is
appropriate, talk about the buyer's rather than your own.

The salesman who has done his homework will never be at a loss
to open the pleasantries, but equally he will firmly but politely try to
steer the discussion round to business matters at the earliest
opportunity.

Opening words Pleasantries out of the way, what next? What should the salesman say?

It is impossible to be definitive about the ultimate choice of words because they will depend upon so many factors: the nature of the service; the situation; the relationship with the buyer, to name but a few.

However, there are a number of tried and tested ways to start the sales call. The salesman can:
— ask a question;
— give new information;
— quote a reference;
— use a sales aid;
— give a demonstration;
— link the call to a previous visit.

What the salesman should *never* use as an opening are tired and apologetic phrases, like:

'I'm sorry to take up your time . . .' (Implying 'What I have to say is quite unimportant'.)

'I was in the area and thought you would want to see me.' (Implying 'I couldn't think of anything better to do'.)

Openings like these diminish the value of both the salesman and his service in the mind of the buyer.

Successful openings

The question

A question can be a good way of making impact at the beginning of the meeting because it will involve the buyer straight away. For example:

'Mr Buyer, is it true that your company is moving out of the city into a rural area?'

'Yes, we hope to move in a year's time.'

'Then you will be interested in the house-hunting service we provide for key workers moving into new areas. It will save you and your staff an awful lot of time and trouble.'

What buyer would not want to hear more?

But take note. The salesman had done his research and by asking the question, obtained the answer he expected. Hence the fluent follow-up.

Giving new information

This opening operates in a similar way to the above. In fact with very little re-phrasing it could become a question.

'Mr Buyer, not many people know this yet, but because we have completely reorganized our distribution system, we can now offer an office stationery service that on average will reduce stockholding in a company of your size by about 20 per cent.'

There are two attention grabbers here. The buyer is being inducted into a small, select group of people who are privy to the new development and the potential savings are well and truly laid on the line.

However, there is an important point to note with this type of opening. The salesman must be able to substantiate his claim by having factual evidence in support.

The reference

There are two types of reference openings, the personal and impersonal. In practice, both of them operate like giving new information above. Taking each in turn:

The personal reference From time to time the salesman will get a new lead from a satisfied customer who suggests that a friend or associate could be interested in the service. When this happens it provides an invaluable opening opportunity.

> 'Hello Mr Buyer, Mr Jones at your other factory was so impressed with our service that he suggested I came to see you to check if it would be possible to achieve similar savings here.'

The impersonal reference It is sometimes possible to show a letter from a satisfied customer or quote from an article in a trade journal or the national press.

> 'Mr Buyer, did you see the article in the city page which rated our personal investment service as the best one for producing capital growth?'

More care has to be taken with the letter reference because the buyer will have to have either heard of the satisfied company or be able to link the relevance of the benefits to his own organization.

If the reference company is different to the buyer's in size, nature of business, market position, technology or in any other significant way, then it is unlikely to impress.

Using sales aids

We mentioned sales aids earlier in this chapter. If a suitable aid is used during the opening it will be certain to gain attention. Aids are particularly effective if used with a question or information opening.

> 'Mr Buyer, look very carefully at this plastic moulding. Would you believe it is off a tool that has been in continuous use for two years? Let me tell you. . . .'

> 'Mr Buyer, this first photograph shows how the office area

looked before we designed a newer and more efficient layout. This one is how it looks today (new photograph). Not only is there more room for the workers, but also. . . .'

When using sales aids such as photographs, the salesman should keep control of them and once they have served their purpose, they should be put away carefully (because they are valuable). It is not good practice to leave sales aids on the desk because they can distract the buyer or, worse still, lead him back to an earlier part of the presentation sequence.

If the sales material is to be left with the buyer, the salesman should use the meeting time to point out the main features of the service and talk about the benefits. The buyer can study the details by reading the literature after the salesman has left.

Demonstrations

As well as full blown demonstrations mentioned earlier in this chapter, which might be seen as special events, it is possible to open a sales call with a different sort of demonstration. Here are two examples:

'Mr Buyer, I would like to demonstrate to you how our pension plan beats any competitive scheme that we know. Now first of all how much would you normally expect to pay. . . .'

'Mr Buyer, let me show you how our service can save you at least £5,000 per year.'

These openings can be particularly potent if the salesman can get the buyer to participate in any calculations that need to be made. In fact, if the salesman can let the buyer take over the calculations, the buyer in effect convinces himself about the value of the service.

Links with earlier visits

A link opening is ideal for keeping up the momentum of the selling process. It could work like this:

> 'Hello, Mr Buyer. Last time I was here I measured up the dimensions of your machine shop. I have now calculated some figures about the energy savings you could expect if. . . .'

Sometimes the onus would be on the buyer to do some extra work between the salesman's visits. In these circumstances the salesman has to politely push for action, without being too aggressive or sarcastic if the buyer has not been able to fulfil his part of the bargain.

Thus 'Any news yet?' is a bit too weak. And 'You promised that by now you would have . . .' could prove to be slightly too challenging.

A better opening might be:

> 'Mr Buyer, when I was here last Friday you said you would be discussing our proposal with the managing director. Well, I have taken the opportunity to go through the figures again and I'm thinking that we could have been rather conservative with some of them. On my new calculations I think the savings could be even greater. . . .'

Hopefully, the managing director has approved the proposal by now after talking to the buyer. But if the buyer hasn't yet been able to meet him, then he won't be feeling too guilty that he has let the salesman down. What is more, the buyer now has an even stronger argument to put before the managing director.

After all this preparation the salesman should be feeling extremely confident as he approaches the meeting with the buyer. Let us recap on the areas he has covered.

He has considered call objectives and from this developed an action plan which concerned itself with:
- putting together a logically sequenced presentation;
- thinking about the most appropriate behaviour;
- supporting materials and visual aids;

– the environment for the meeting;
– the best way to open the meeting.
   He now sets out for the meeting.

Arrival

The salesman should plan to arrive in plenty of time. This will be doubly important for visits to new customers or new locations when time might be lost trying to park the car or locating the buyer's office. The last thing he wants to do is to arrive hot and flustered after parking on double yellow lines and having sprinted the last few hundred yards to make the appointment on time.

Even worse is for the salesman to arrive late. In these circumstances he might not even be seen.

It is good practice to plan to arrive 10–15 minutes before the appointed time, even earlier for new or particularly important customers. This also means making due allowance for traffic conditions or delays due to roadworks.

Meeting the buyer

The long awaited moment arrives and the salesman is at last face-to-face with the buyer. He introduces himself, remembering to smile, use eye contact and a firm handshake. He uses the buyer's name.

He only sits down when invited to do so and leads into pleasantries with a view to getting down to business at the first opportunity.

Then the opening words just as he planned . . .

Nothing can possibly go wrong now . . . or can it? Unfortunately yes. Several things can still spoil the meeting.

Spoilers

Personal appearance

Since this has already been stressed, suffice it to say that an inappropriate personal appearance could well lead a buyer to assume that neither the salesman nor his company or services are appropriate.

Time wasting

Buyers are busy people and it is unlikely they will want to waste their time on small talk.

We have already stated that as a general rule pleasantries should be kept to a minimum. This also applies to telling the latest joke; giving a stroke by stroke account of the weekend's golf match (even if you holed in one); or what you think about the state of the nation.

There are only two exceptions to this rule:

1　When the buyer clearly wants to indulge in small talk (and even then it is worth remembering that he is wasting your time).
2　If it seems appropriate to do so at the end of the meeting *after* the business has been concluded.

Drinking

However appropriate or sociable it might seem at the time, it is difficult to conceal the fact that alcohol has been drunk. There is nothing particularly wrong with this except that if other calls have to be made, it should be remembered that not everyone approves. Moreover, alcohol smells on the breath and this can be particularly offensive to a customer, especially if the meeting is taking place in a confined space or poorly-ventilated office.

Equally dangerous is the fact that drinking can easily slow reactions and impair judgment, whereas the salesman needs all his wits about him when he is in a selling situation.

If in the course of his business the salesman is expected to entertain he should drink with caution.

Not thinking about the buyer and his needs

This is perhaps the biggest spoiler of them all, because many salesmen are unaware of it. To rectify the situation:
— let the buyer talk when he wants to;
— don't interrupt;
— listen to what he says;
— talk about him and his situation;
— ask his advice;
— don't pressurize him;
— don't talk down to him;
— don't try to mislead him with unsubstantiated claims.

Summary

The salesman's objectives in the opening moments of the interview are to:
— gain the attention of the buyer;
— arouse his interest;
— begin to build confidence.
    The pre-call planning described in this chapter should help him to achieve these objectives quickly. Failure to do so will seriously put at risk the remainder of the sales interview.

Application questions

1 Which sales sequence do you follow? What are its strengths and weaknesses?

2 Are there any mnemonics, key sentences or other means which you can think of that might help you to achieve your objectives?

3 What supporting materials, sales literature, demonstration material or visual aids do you use? How do you use them? Can

they be improved in any way?

4 How do you handle the pleasantries at the beginning of a sales interview? Do you find it difficult to move on to business matters? Which opening technique(s) do you prefer to use?

5 What 'spoilers' do you object to when you observe them in other salesmen? What, for you personally, might be an area to which you should pay particular attention?

Exercises

Exercise 3.1:   *A confident approach*

Opening the sales interview is perhaps the most critical phase of our meeting with the customer. If we get off to a good start it sets the tone for the whole of the meeting. Unfortunately the reverse of this is also true. How then do we ensure that we get off to a good start? Well, first of all we have to look and feel confident in the way we conduct ourselves. If we look uncertain and worried then it undermines all of our planning and preparatory work. Second, we have to say the right things and gain control of the interview (but more about that later, in the next exercise). For now we will examine the issue of confidence. What is it that some salesmen *do* that creates an air of confidence? What do you think are the important factors that contribute to one's confidence? How can you measure confidence? The answer to these and other questions should hopefully become clearer when you have completed this exercise.

1 Prepare six pieces of plain card approximately to the size of playing cards and number them one to six.
2 Think of six salesmen you know fairly well. They might be existing colleagues, people you have worked with in the past, or

even people who have sold things to you. Write their names or initials on the six cards.

3 Shuffle the six cards and then 'deal' three at random in front of you. Using these three cards, decide in which ways any two of the salesmen depicted on them are different from the third in terms of how they exhibit confidence. For example you might decide that two of them tend to be very relaxed, while the third is always tense. Alternatively, it might be that one demonstrates technical wizardry while the other two are merely competent. There are no right or wrong answers, the choice is your own.

Note: In this exercise we are focusing on behaviour (what people do), therefore avoid differences based on physical characteristics such as build, colour, etc.

4 When you have differentiated between the first pair and the single one, enter your observations on Worksheet 1, where it is marked 'Shuffle 1'.

5 Re-shuffle the cards and deal another three at random and again identify a behaviour characteristic of two of the salesmen that differentiates them from the third. Enter the results on Worksheet 1 in the next space down the page 'Shuffle 2'. Do not repeat the behaviour characteristics you identified above but strive to find a new dimension of confidence each time.

6 Repeat this process with new, randomly selected sets of three cards until Worksheet 1 is completed.

7 Looking at the set of eight behaviour characteristics which you have constructed on Worksheet 1, now rank them in order of importance. Again, there are no right or wrong answers because this ranking is all to do with your own beliefs and values.

Note: Use an alphabetical code for ranking. A being the most important.

8 Transpose the information on Worksheet 1 to Worksheet 2 taking care to observe the following:

(a) The confident behaviours listed in rank order with what you consider to be most important at the top of the list.

Worksheet 1: Concepts of confidence

Shuffle	With confident behaviour in mind, what do the pair of salesmen have in common?	With confident behaviour in mind, what makes the other saleman different?	*Ranking*
1			
2			
3			
4			
5			
6			
7			
8			

Note: Remember to describe just one aspect of the salesmen's behaviour each time

(b) The most effective behaviour characteristics, whether demonstrated by the pair or the single salesman, are entered in the boxes on the left-hand side of the page.

9 Take item A (the one you have rated as the most important behaviour characteristic) and now rate each of the salesmen using the rating code shown at the bottom of the worksheet. It is generally found helpful if the best salesman is chosen and rated 1, then the least effective who is rated 5. The others, naturally, fall between these two limits or 'poles'. In this example the salesman depicted on Card 3 was the best and Card 6 was the least effective. The others fall between these two limits as shown, e.g.

	Card numbers							
Effective behaviour	1	2	3	4	5	6	Self	Less effective behaviour
A		2	3	1	3	4	5		

10 Complete the scoring of Item A by rating yourself on the same scale as that used for the salesmen. Enter your score in the column headed 'Self'.

11 Score all the other elements of confident behaviour B to H, in a similar way.

12 Study the completed Worksheet 2 very carefully and answer these questions, making notes as you do so.

(a) What behaviour demonstrated confidence in these salesmen?

(b) Which of these are the most important?

(c) Where are your own strengths (low scores in self column).

(d) Which are the behaviours you will need to practise more if you are to convcy confidence more readily to customers? (High scores.)

(e) How might you practise these behaviours? (Write down ideas you may have e.g. try something different at my next

Worksheet 2: *Rating of confidence*

	Effective behaviour	1	2	3	4	5	6	Self	Less effective behaviour
A									
B									
C									
D									
E									
F									
G									
H									

Rating code:	1	2	3	4	5
	Most effective	Above average	Average	Below average	Least effective

sales interview, try role playing a sales interview with a friend or colleague using this new behaviour etc.)

Exercise 3.2:   *The opening statement*

On the following Worksheet 3 are listed a number of sales situations which could easily be encountered in day-to-day work. Your task is to imagine that you are actually faced with these situations and to respond to them accordingly.

As we have seen in Chapter 3 each sales interview will invariably commence with some exchange of pleasantries. However, *for the purpose* of this exercise, assume that the pleasantries phase is over and your opening statement will be the first move in the business transaction.

When you have responded to *all* the situations outlined in Worksheet 3, turn to page 228 to check your answers. It is important to remember that it is impossible to be absolutely prescriptive about sales situations such as those described in this exercise. Thus the 'answers' are there in the nature of guidelines, with brief notes to commend them. It will be most unlikely that you come up with exactly the same formulation of words, but if your overall approach is along similar lines, then you should be getting the interview started in a reasonable manner with every prospect of subsequent success.

Worksheet 3

Imagine that the pleasantries are over and you are about to open these individual and unrelated sales interviews. What would you say? Write your answers on a separate sheet of paper.

Situation   1:   You are visiting a client on the heels of an advertising campaign in the national press.

Situation   2:   It is your first meeting with the client.

Situation   3:   You have submitted a proposal to the client company.

Situation   4:   Your organization has developed a new service.

Situation   5:   Your contact at the company has been loath to commit himself to a decision despite several earlier meetings.

Situation   6:   There has been a complaint to head office.

Situation   7:   You are asked to visit a client company at the request of their buyer.

Situation   8:   The buyer is an extremely busy person.

Situation   9:   You were given a referral to the client by another customer.

Situation 10:   You want to establish a long-term contract with an established client.

Exercise 3.3:   Listening

Throughout the sales interview the salesman will have to listen carefully to how the client responds to his presentation. As Chapter 3 suggests, the more the salesman is under stress at the interview the more he worries about himself and his feelings. In these circumstances 'good listening' becomes a low priority, not intentionally, but as all his resources are diverted into self-protection, there is little energy left over for listening. This exercise is designed to give you some insights about how good a listener you might be and if necessary provide you with some ideas about ways to develop your listening skills.

Worksheet 4 gives a series of statements at the two ends of a scale. Mark an X on the scale in a position that equated with where you see yourself.

Worksheet 4: Listening

1 When listening I concentrate mainly on picking up facts and figures.

When listening I try to understand the underlying meaning about what is being said.

2 If there is an external noise I would ask to close an open window to reduce it.

If there is an external noise I wouldn't bother to try to reduce it.

3 When a person says something that captures my imagination I get very enthusiastic and vociferous.

When a person says something that captures my imagination I try to stay on his wavelength and see where it is leading.

4 When I am not sure that I have understood I ask a question to check.

When I am not sure that I have understood I often feign that I have by nodding.

5 I prefer to keep eye contact at the expense of taking notes.

I prefer to take notes at the expense of keeping eye contact.

6 I find I can make an early judgement about whether a speaker is going to be interesting or boring.

I find it difficult to make an early judgement about whether a speaker is going to be interesting or boring.

7 I find other people's mannerisms most distracting while they are talking.

I am often not aware of the speaker's mannerisms until someone points them out to me.

8 While driving the car or relaxing at home, I prefer listening to music or light entertainment.

While driving the car or relaxing at home, I prefer listening to serious debates or documentary programmes.

9 If somebody keeps using slogans, jargon or words that are in conflict with my value system I try to understand why they do it.

I get annoyed if somebody keeps using slogans, jargon or words that conflict with my value system.

10 I find I am more concerned about what a person says rather than how he says it.

I find I am more concerned about how a person speaks rather than what he is saying.

Now check your answers on page 231.

Example

| when listening I am picking out all the facts | A ———×——— | B ——— | when listening I try to understand the underlying meaning of what is being said |

In this example the X at postion A indicates that this listener has a strong tendency to listen out for facts. Had the X been at position B, it would show that the listener tends to be less strong at listening for facts but tries harder to understand what the speaker is really getting at, even if at the sacrifice of a few facts.

Exercise 3.4: '*A day in the life of . . .*'

The business of opening the sales interview as we have already seen depends upon the salesman being confident and saying the right things. There are however, another set of factors to consider – the logistics of getting from one appointment to another on time and the so-called 'spoilers' that were mentioned in Chapter 3. Almost all of these can be overcome by a salesman who is determined to be successful.

This exercise asks you to look at a day in the life of an anonymous salesman. Perhaps at first sight it might seem a bit 'far fetched', but we know from experience that every event listed has once happened to salesmen we have met. True, they are unlikely to happen all on the same day as with our anonymous salesman, but the fact that they happen at all suggests that there is always room for improvement.

Read the following 'case study' carefully and then answer the questions that accompany it.

7.30   Alarm clock rings as usual. I do feel tired, smashing party last night but perhaps we should have left earlier. Think I'll have to cut down a bit on the drinking, I don't feel too bright. Think I'll treat myself to a five minute lay in.

8.15   Damn. I dropped off again. I'd better get a move on now. I'm late.

8.20   Oh No! Why is it you always cut yourself shaving on a day when you're going to be busy.

8.30   No time for breakfast. A swift cup of tea though . . . ah . . . nectar! Where's my case? What did I do with those brochures? Diary? Glad I thought of that, it's in my other jacket pocket.

8.45   Sit in car, wait for children to take them to school. Check on day's schedule. Oh blast it! I'd forgotten old Smithers at Prescott Engineering had been taken ill. How shall I fill in till 11.00 when I see Fredericks. Never mind, I'll think of something. Take children to school.

9.05   Now let's see who can I visit instead of Smithers. Got it, that chap, whatshisname Edwards at Trusty Tubing. I'll take a chance and try him. I haven't been there for a while.

9.30   I know they are on this industrial estate somewhere.

9.40   Well I'm blowed. Fancy them going out of business, never thought that would happen. 'Thank you for that information sir!'

9.45   I'll have to see someone having travelled this far. I'll try a couple of cold calls while I'm here.

10.15   Well, that was a waste of time. How was I to know that they have no need for our service and that first lot! How can it possibly take them twenty minutes before they can find out there is nobody who can see me. Talk about inefficiency. Better push off to Fredericks, he's expecting me at 11.00 and he's a bit of a stickler for punctuality.

10.30   Would you believe it! Roadworks here of all places. Let's try a bit of music on the radio. Isn't that typical? They always broadcast about traffic jams when you're actually stuck in one.

10.40   This won't do, nothing is moving. I'd better try the back doubles.

11.15   'Sorry I'm late Mr Fredericks. Blasted roadworks!' He looks a bit crusty. I'd better get straight into my spiel. Now, what was that smashing opening I thought of last night at the party? . . . ah, I remember . . . 'Any news yet about that quotation I submitted after my last visit, Mr Fredericks?' He looks bland and says he rang Head Office with a query – hadn't I heard? I tell him we keep getting cock ups whenever Head Office gets involved. Ask about the query. Don't fully understand it. I think I'll get the Sales Manager on to it – about time he got out and did a bit of work. I promise to sort out the query.

12.00 Next appointment. Jim Sutcliff at the Red Lion Hotel. I'll get there a bit early and relax.

12.15 Have a pint and idly look through the situations vacant column in the paper – you never know your luck.

12.30 Jim arrives. He's great fun, easily the friendliest company I visit. Order some more drinks.

13.00 Excellent lunch. A superb 'Chateauneuf-du-Pape' and I must say a brandy and cigar really do finish the meal off nicely. Thought the bill was a bit steep though, still that's what the expense account is for. One good thing about meeting Jim is that I always stock up with enough jokes to keep me going 'till the next time I see him.

14.30 As I leave Jim in the car park, he tells me that he will try to get his MD to look at our latest proposal. Not such a bad day after all.

14.50 Luckily I saw the police car following and slowed down. Wouldn't want to get pinched for speeding. They'd probably have breathalysed me after that lunch. On time for my next appointment too.

15.25 Without wishing to boast, I reckon I was pretty good at Lights 'n Lamps. Didn't miss a trick. Still it's probably too early to get an order there on just the second visit. Must remember to take our new catalogue next time. I'd left it at home.

15.30 Beginning to feel a bit rough. I think it's probably last night's party and the lunch catching up with me. I did make a bit of a pig of myself with the 'tornedos Rossini'. Mind you, I didn't have any breakfast. I'll look out for a chemist shop and get something to settle my stomach.

15.40 It's no good I think I've got a touch of 'Rossini's Revenge'. I'll phone to cancel my last appointment and get home quickly.

16.15 Arrive home. Wouldn't you know it. The washing machine's gone wrong and flooded the kitchen. I help out with the mopping up operation.

16.45 Just time to phone round to make a few appointments. Wish the kids would keep quiet. Now someone's hammering on the front door.

17.15 Make out some call reports. I'd better make the cold calls sound a bit more interesting than they really were. Still, no one will be any wiser.

18.00 That's funny. I've just realized my rumbling tum feels better. Hadn't noticed through all the chaos since I've been home. I feel quite peckish.

18.15 Nice to sit down with the family for tea, even if it is a bit late.

19.30 Settle down to watch TV.

23.00 I meant to get to bed a bit earlier but I thought I'd have another look through the paper. Tell the wife I've seen a job advertised that looks better paid than my present one. She thinks I ought to apply for it. Think I will. It's been a busy day, that's for sure.

Questions

1 If you were this man's manager, would you really want him to be on your staff?

2 Being brutally honest with yourself, have you ever (or do you ever) experienced the type of events that happen in this case study?

3 What actions might you take to avoid the pitfalls illustrated in this case study, such as:

(a) Making better use of your time.
(b) Showing more loyalty to your company.
(c) Becoming more motivated and keeping a positive attitude.
(d) Keeping in better physical shape.
(e) Not putting your job at risk, e.g. through speeding.
(f) Being better prepared for meetings.

Write down all the actions you could take which would be beneficial.

Note: A full critique of this case study is provided on page 234.

Exercise 3.5:   The George Reeves story

In the previous exercise we saw how a poor salesman's day can become a chapter of accidents, most of which are self-inflicted. Here is a story about another salesman, George Reeves. After reading it, write down your answers to the following questions.

1 Was George Reeves genuinely lucky?
2 What distinguishes George Reeves from the salesman in Exercise 3.4?
3 What personal learning points might there be for you from the George Reeves story?

When you have written your answers to these questions, check with those given on page 236.

George Reeves is in his middle forties. For the past two years he has been working as an independent management consultant specializing in career counselling and staff development. As George puts it, 'What I am doing now is a culmination of all the years I worked for other companies. Although I learned a tremendous amount about ways of sorting out "people" problems, working within the constraints of one's employer company always limited my freedom to act in the way I thought best. Now, thank goodness, I am free to propose any course of action that I think will make impact on a client company's problem. If they don't like my suggestions, then I don't get the contract. It's as simple as that.'

George has been successful in his new venture, not only in financial terms but also in terms of personal satisfaction. As he maintains, 'I'm now doing the sort of work I really believe in – it's great!'

A few months ago George attended a family wedding. It was the first time for years that the vast network of relatives had all assembled in one place.

He was particularly interested to meet his cousin Richard Storey again. Although they had been very close as children and shared a passion for cricket, they hadn't seen each other for something like thirty years. Much water had flowed under their respective bridges in the intervening time.

Richard, it turned out, had left school and had embarked upon a career in commerce. He was now a senior executive with a leading financial group in the City. Naturally enough, while enjoying the conviviality of the occasion, both men brought each other up to date about their personal situations, both family and careerwise.

Afterwards, George wondered if he had gone a little over the top in his conversation with Richard. He reflected how his natural enthusiasm for his work, doubtless fuelled by champagne, had probably caused him to 'go on a bit' about some of the assignments he had undertaken and the results he had achieved. Nevertheless, he was comforted by the fact that Richard had seemed interested in what he had said.

Imagine his surprise, when a few days later he received a telephone call from Peter Jackson, the Personnel Director of Richard's company.

'Mr Reeves, I hope you don't mind me calling but I've just been talking to your cousin Richard Storey. He was telling me how impressed he was to hear about work you have been doing and we both think that probably you could help us. Can we meet and talk?'

The meeting took place. Reeves and Jackson took an instant liking to each other and after several lengthy discussions it was agreed that Reeves' services would be used to assess the company's management development needs and to run a series of development programmes for selected key personnel.

The company were most pleased with the outcome of this work.

If you spoke to him today, George Reeves will tell you that this particular project was 'a pure stroke of luck . . . I hadn't planned it or anything!'

Do you think that George was lucky, or is he being unduly modest?

4

Benefit Selling

Overview

Customers do not buy a service, but rather they seek to acquire a range of benefits that a service will bring them. Every service has descriptive technical features which might differentiate it from competing services. However, the salesman will be concerned to translate these features into customer benefits. It is these benefits he sells rather than the service itself.

A simple formula, the expression '*which means that*', can be used to link a benefit to a feature.

The salesman should make a comprehensive analysis of the service and his company, and in doing so identify all the features and benefits. In practice benefits fall into three categories: standard benefits (which arise from the nature of the service); company benefits (which arise from the nature of the supplying company, such as the quality of its staff, its reputation and so on); and differential benefits (which arise from advantageous differences the supplier has over its competitors).

Not all benefits are equally valuable for all customers, and so the salesman has to identify their customer appeal and then frame his offer specifically around those appropriate benefits with the highest appeal. A benefit analysis form shows how the salesman can prepare his best offer.

To talk of benefits is not enough. The discriminating buyer would expect any claim the salesman might make to be substantiated.

Finally, this chapter looks at the communication process and puts forward a set of simple rules that a salesman can use to improve his communication skills.

Benefit selling

In Chapter 3 we introduced the mnemonic A.B.C. with the claim that it prompted one of the best sequences for a successful sales interview . . . Attention, Benefits, Close.

The remainder of that chapter then went on to examine the various ways that the salesman could gain attention and at the same time work at developing the buyer's confidence.

Clearly the opening techniques the salesman uses are instrumental in setting the tone for the whole interview. But having gained that initial attention, the salesman then has to progress to the next stage of the sequence, selling the benefits of his service.

Simultaneously, he will have to continue the confidence-building process he has started at the opening phase of the meeting.

Benefit selling – what does it mean?

When somebody uses the services of, for example, a surveyor as they contemplate moving into a new house, it is self-evident that there is no altruistic motivation on their part to preserve surveyors as a species. No, their reasoning is far more basic: 'If I'm going to make a huge investment in this property, I want to know that it is not going to fall down around my ears'. It is their own security and interest they are safeguarding.

A manufacturer made this same point more pungently when he observed, 'Last year we sold one million quarter-inch drills, not because people wanted quarter-inch drills, but because they wanted quarter-inch holes'.

This statement encapsulates a basic principle of successful selling: that purchasers are not motivated in the first instance by the physical features or attributes of a service or a product, but by the benefits that those features or attributes bring with them. There are examples of this principle in operation all around us.

The company that uses an employment agency for all of its recruitment is buying a bundle of benefits associated with getting its manpower needs met without tying its own staff down in the administration of lengthy recruitment and selection procedures.

We buy insurance because we believe it will provide financial security for our families and loved ones.

The company that uses an office cleaning service does so because it is found to be more convenient and less costly than having to employ its own cleaning staff and ensure that they are supervised after normal working hours.

The difference between the service itself and the benefits it supplies to customers is not just a question of semantics. It is at the very heart of successful selling.

The salesman, recognizing that people buy the service for what it will do for them, will need to point out to customers the benefits they will receive from the service rather than spend his time explaining its features or how it works.

It is so easy for the salesman to forget that he is an expert about his particular service, whether it is banking, insurance, business consultancy or whatever. Being an expert, there is a great temptation for him to demonstrate his knowledge and skill by talking about the technical details and minutiae of his particular service. It can sound so impressive; but is it what the customer really wants to hear? Clearly the answer is no.

At times it might be important for the customer to have a modicum of technical knowledge, at least enough to satisfy his curiosity or to enable him to convince his colleagues that this particular service is exactly what they are looking for. Generally, though, he is looking for the benefits. The successful salesman realizes this and quickly translates the technicalities into customer benefits. He does it like this.

Each time he describes a technical feature or some other attribute of the service, he will use a simple formula to ensure that the customer benefit is not overlooked. He will use the phrase '*which means that'* to link the feature with the benefit it brings. Although this might sound somewhat contrived, in practice it works very easily and in no way causes the salesman's dialogue to become stilted or lose its fluency. Here are some examples:

> 'We have the largest advertizing budget of any local estate agent, *which means that* we sell your house more quickly.'

> 'We specialize in arranging car insurance for mature drivers with a proven safety record, *which means that* our premiums are very much lower than other less discriminating companies.'

> 'We have some of the most up-to-date equipment in the country, *which means that* the printing we undertake is of the highest quality.'

This, then, is what is meant by benefit selling. Whenever the salesman mentions a special feature of his service he should always go on to tell the customer what benefits he will receive from that feature.

If the salesman cannot think of a positive benefit, then that feature can hardly be worth talking about and should be dropped from his presentation.

The successful salesman, therefore, identifies a whole range of customer benefits that can be derived from using the service.

Identifying benefits

The salesman identifies benefits by being extremely analytical about his company and the services it provides. He will list as many features as he possibly can and then translate each of them into customer benefits. From the resulting comprehensive list of potential benefits, it becomes a relatively easy task, when facing the buyer, to select those specific benefits that have an appeal to him.

As with the sales sequence, the salesman cannot conduct the interview with a list in his hand. Therefore he needs to practise memorizing all these benefits and become fluent at connecting the right benefit with each feature.

In practice it will be found that benefits fall into three categories.

1 Standard benefits

These are the basic benefits that arise from the features of the company and its services. They might not be particularly unique or earth-shattering, but put yourself in the buyer's shoes for a few moments. What might seem dull and obvious to the salesman could well be news for the buyer who is meeting him for the first time. Even if the salesman knows that every competing company could claim the same standard benefits, he should still have them on his comprehensive list.

Buyers are not always as knowledgeable as they might claim to be, so if the salesman overlooked telling a buyer about one of the standard benefits, that buyer might assume, quite wrongly, that the particular service compared unfavourably with competing services.

Indeed the sale might well go to a competitor who took the trouble to include standard benefits in his offer.

Sometimes a standard benefit can lead to an opening for another benefit. The so-called 'double benefit' operates like this.

'We will give your company overdraft facilities, *which means that*:
— you will no longer have to be so worried about your cash flow position;
— your suppliers can maintain their scheduled deliveries with confidence.'

In the example the first benefit is clearly to the customer's advantage. The second one has implications of continuity of production, which can benefit both the customer and his suppliers.

2   Company benefits

Whenever a customer buys a service, he is simultaneously buying into a relationship with the supplier. Links will be forged between the two at many levels. For example, their accounts departments will be in contact to deal with payment or financial matters; people on installation work or after sales servicing will interact with the personnel at the buyer's company; delivery men with storemen; designers with technicians, and so on.

Quite naturally, the buyer needs to have confidence in the supplying company. He will be concerned about its reputation, the quality of its staff, its willingness to be flexible and its ability to provide what it promises.

With this in mind, the salesman must be certain to include benefits pertaining to the company and its back-up services in his identification of benefits.

Typical company benefits might be:

'Most of our clients are small but developing companies like yours, *which means that* we have tremendous expertise in understanding the financial problems associated with rapid growth, *which means that* we are well-equipped to help you.'

'We are part of a multi-national group *which means that* we can provide this identical service in any country in the world.'

Sometimes the expression *which means that* can become rather clumsy. When this happens often a neater linking word is *because*.

'You can be sure of personal attention from us *because* we are a small family business.'

It is even possible to use *which means that* and *because* together:

'This particular loan scheme operates over a 4–10 year period, *which means that* it is particularly suitable for the purchase of fixed assets such as company cars, plant or equipment *because* the period of the loan will be virtually the same as the life of the asset.'

3   Differential benefits

Throughout the sales interview the salesman will be trying to convince the buyer of the benefits of using his company's service.

While standard benefits and company benefits might be enough to win the buyer's conviction, the probability is that by themselves they will not. This is because in a competitive marketplace most suppliers vying for the business will not be able to claim standard or company benefits that, in truth, differ much from those of their rivals.

However, if the seller can identify a benefit that cannot be matched by his competitors, then this clearly gives him an advantage over them. Benefits that provide this competitive edge over rivals are known as differential benefits.

It is most important for the salesman to identify these, because they alone enable the company to establish a unique position among suppliers. Ultimately it is this uniqueness that will be the launching pad for sales success.

Every salesman should be able to identify differential benefits about his company and its services. It might be difficult to do, but it is an essential pre-requisite to a successful sales interview.
(NOTE: If the salesman cannot identify any differential benefits, he is in fact implying that *in all respects* his company and service is identical to those of a competitor. It seems most improbable that this could ever be true.)

Here are some examples of differential benefits:

'We are the only supplier with the resources and systems to be able to provide you with a round-the-clock service, *which means that* you get 100 per cent cover from us.'

'We actually own the patents for this cleaning process, *which means that* we know more about it than anyone else, *which means that* you get the best possible service.'

Customer appeal

When the salesman has identified all the benefits associated with his company and its service, it will become clear that not all of the listed benefits will have the same impact on all buyers.

For example, some buyers will be concerned more about benefits associated with price and availability, while others will want reassurance on quality and reliability.

The successful salesman, therefore, uses a benefit analysis sheet, like the one shown on page 135, and works through it, collecting together all the relevant facts for each of his customers.

In this way he builds up a collection of tailor-made features and benefits that will have a high level of customer appeal for each of his clients.

The first column on the benefit analysis sheet is in fact headed 'customer appeal'. The purpose of this is to help determine what issues are of particular concern for the customer.

It is advisable to use an intermediate stage in the benefit analysis process because the apparently intellectually simple task of relating benefits to features usually proves extremely difficult the first time a salesman tries it. Thus, the process would start with the feature,

Feature	Advantage	Benefit
(What the product is, or is made from)	(What it does)	(What the customer gets that he needs)
Teflon	Non-stick	Trouble-free cooking Quicker washing-up Better presentation of food, etc.
Access credit card	Provides credit facilities all over the world	Eliminates the need to carry large amounts of cash Eases cash flow problems, etc.

Figure 9

would then go on to describe the advantage of the feature, and would finish with the benefit itself.

To make this process easier to understand, study the examples given in Figure 9.

Ask questions to determine what constitutes customer appeal

The salesman should be prepared to ask questions to find out and confirm the buyer's need. Until he has done so, he will remain quite unaware of the customer's main concerns.

The best questions to ask are those that cannot be answered with a 'yes' or a 'no', the so-called open questions.

Thus, while questions like:

'Are you satisfied with your existing supplier?'

might provide some information because they invite 'yes' or 'no' as an answer, they are more likely to lead to a discussion in which the buyer feels he is under intense interrogation.

The open question invariably reveals more useful data to the salesman and yet comes over with far less aggression. These questions always begin with words like What? How? When? Who? Where?

For example:

'How do you see the company coping with storage when the production consistently reaches the new output targets, Mr Buyer?'

In answering such a question, the buyer will convey very much more information than had a 'yes' or 'no' reply been given.

Here are other examples of the open question:

'When would be the best time to start a pilot run using our service, Mr Buyer?'

'What results would have to be achieved to convince your colleagues that our service really works, Mr Buyer?'

Establishing commitment

Questions can also help the salesman to establish how committed the buyer is to his proposition.

It has been found that the more the buyer can be persuaded to agree with the salesman, the more his confidence in the salesman is increased and the higher his commitment becomes.

Thus when he explains benefits, the salesman uses the opportunity to confirm the buyer's interest and increase his commitment.

To do this he might phrase his questions as follows:

'When we are able to offer a 24-hour service in the way that no competing company can, you have to agree it is most impressive, don't you, Mr Buyer?'

'. . . Our tool repair service can therefore reduce your machine downtime and your maintenance costs in the way I've just described. This is what you are looking for Mr Buyer, isn't it?'

Proof

It is good practice to be able to substantiate any claim with some evidence or proof. This may be in the form of a technical report, an independent survey, a newspaper article, a photograph, a letter from a satisfied customer, a performance graph, and so on.

The benefit analysis preparation provides an opportunity to consider what proof is required to back up a benefit statement as the completed benefit analysis sheet on pages 136 and 137 shows.

The 'so what?' test

To determine that the benefit statements derived from the benefit

Example of benefit analysis sheet

Customer _____ Services(s) required _____

Customer appeal	Features	Advantages	Benefits	Proof
What issues are of particular concern for this customer? e.g. cost reliability availability safety simplicity etc.	What features of the service can best illustrate these issues? What are they? How do they work?	What advantages do these features provide? i.e. what do they do for the customer?	How can the tangible benefits for this customer be expressed to give maximum customer appeal? i.e. what does the customer get THAT HE NEEDS?	What evidence can be provided to back up the claim that this benefit can be realized?

Example of a completed benefit analysis sheet

Customer – XYZ Ltd　　　　Service(s) Required – Management Training Courses

Customer appeal	Features	Advantages	Benefits	Proof
The training must be practical rather than theoretical	We only use management theories that have come from authenticated research in industry	You do not get the tutor's pet theories or the latest 'fad'	Your trainees learn about the best practices from the best companies and so become better managers	Examples of research studies. Typical programme course notes
	Our course leaders have been managers themselves	They know what will work in practice and what won't	Your trainees learn things they can actually apply at work and get results	Career experience of tutors. Students' remarks
The training must make the best use of the time available	We insist that trainees complete some prework before they arrive on a course	They arrive prepared. Their interest is aroused	No time is wasted before getting down to the important issues	Examples of prework
	Our courses are tightly structured	This creates a discipline for both the tutor and trainees	The objectives of the course are achieved in the most cost-effective	Examples of comments from client companies

	We ask trainees to work on case studies or private study in the evenings	Each day is in effect extended by 2–3 hours	It helps to consolidate their learning by getting them to apply the theory in a training environment where they can learn from their mistakes	Examples of typical case study or directed study
The training must produce results	We have a special way of linking the course back to the work situation	Your trainees plan how they will introduce improvements while on the course	Because they are planned, the improvements take place	Examples of action plans
	We have a one day review with trainees 10 weeks after the course to check what has happened	This maintains the momentum generated by the course	Trainees work hard to reach their 'improvement' goals	Evaluation Results from other companies List of satisfied clients

analysis are indeed genuine and not features or advantages masquerading as benefits, we recommend that the 'So what?' test is used. This is how it works.

Using the example of the completed benefit analysis sheet on pages 136 and 137, read down the list of features and after each one ask the question: 'So what?' This is exactly the question that goes through the customer's mind as the salesman makes his presentation. What a conversation stopper! One suddenly realizes that the carefully designed features of the service make very little real impact on the buyer in the face of the question.

Now switch to the advantages column on the benefit analysis sheet and submit each of these to the 'So what?' test. You will experience a very similar result to the above, a resounding 'plop'.

Finally, address the 'So what?' question to each of the listed benefit statements. Immediately it can be seen that a different quality of response is required. The customer cannot really use the 'So what?' question here because each of the benefits are pay-offs that correlate to known areas of customer appeal.

Always remember to use the 'So what?' test whenever you work through a benefit analysis for your particular service.

Communicating benefits

Important though this process of benefit analysis and establishing customer appeal is, its ultimate value depends very much upon the ability of the salesman to communicate these benefits to the buyer.

Unless the salesman can learn to talk 'the buyer's language', he might find that all his preparatory work is of little value.

Most of us can improve our communication skills if we pay attention to what we say and follow a few simple rules.

1 *Keep it simple* – if one word will do, do not use two. Simplicity is one of the best tools of the good communicator. Unfortunately there seems to be a tendency for people to make things sound more complicated than they need to be.

Here are some typical examples:
— 'human resources', meaning 'people';
— 'manufacturing facility', meaning 'factory';
— 'malfunction indicator', meaning 'warning light';
— 'localized capacity deficiency', meaning 'bottleneck';
— 'negative response', meaning 'no';
— 'manual dysfunctional override', meaning 'stop-button'.

Generally speaking, the shorter word or expression will be the better one to use.

2 *Do not use jargon* – technical jargon is great . . . if both parties are familiar with it. But as a general rule, jargon should be used with care. It's easy to see why.

If the customer does not know the latest technical expressions, or is uncertain about what they mean, then the salesman's continual use of them can become very irritating and confusing.

There is also a possibility of showing up senior non-technical sales contacts in front of their junior, but more technically aware, colleagues.

3 *Avoid value words* – the words we use in daily conversation can tell an observer much about us and our value systems.

The salesman in his interview with the buyer needs to be aware of words he might use which could be perceived as an attack on the buyer's values.

We say	They say
Freedom fighter	Terrorist
Ingenious plan	Hair-brained scheme
Clear-sighted	Tunnel vision
Receptive to new ideas	Plagiarist
Enthusiastic support	Shouting mob

The use of some words can be strongly emotional and can prejudice and distract the listener.

4 *Be positive* – the use of active, rather than passive, verbs tends to produce a more positive construction in what we say.

Thus 'We serve the nation' is better than 'The nation is served by us'.

Similarly, putting what we want to emphasize at the beginning of a sentence makes more impact on the listener than if it were put at the end.

'The range of applications of your computer is expanded considerably because of the flexibility of our programmes.'

has a greater effect than

'Because our programmes are so flexible, they expand considerably the range of applications of your computer.'

5 *Avoid using negatives* – 'We will succeed' is better than 'We won't fail'.
6 *Appeal to as many senses as possible* – when we talked about sales aids we pointed out that we use all five senses in communication.
   The more hearing, sight, touch, taste and smell are used in combination, the more powerfully the message is communicated.
7 *Environment* – select the environment most likely to enhance the communication process. As a general rule try to avoid meeting places where there will be too much noise or other distractions, such as people continually walking in and out of the office.
   At all times try to talk to the customer as an equal, because if you have done your homework right, he needs you and your service, just as much as you need him and his business.
   This 'equal status' is often helped by the physical arrangements of the meeting room. For example, it will be easier to talk to the buyer if you both sit at a small coffee table, than if he remains behind a huge desk.

Summary

Customers do not buy the service, they buy the benefits that the service will bring them.

Salesmen must therefore:

— identify the benefits associated with their company and their services;
— make a sales offer in terms of those benefits;
— ask questions to gain responses about customer appeal and commitment to the service;
— communicate clearly, concisely and effectively.

Application questions

1 Think of the main service you offer customers. Identify the standard benefits associated with it. Identify the company benefits. Identify the differential benefits. Which benefits have most appeal to your major customers?

2 What sort of questions do you use to: Identify the buyer's needs? Obtain commitments from the buyer? In the light of the text, are there better questions you might now ask?

3 Choose an example of your company literature. What is its message? How clearly is this communicated? Is the language and layout clear and concise? Is the message the 'correct' one from the customer's viewpoint? Do you have any suggestions that will improve the presentation of the message?

4 In which ways might your sales offer incorporate an appeal to the five senses (hearing, sight, touch, taste and smell), thereby improving its communication prospects?

Exercises

Exercise 4.1: Benefit selling

It is often said that benefit selling is an attitude of mind. The salesman should not sell a service, but rather the benefits that investing in that service will bring to the customer.

Equally, while it might be useful to point out special features of the service or the supplying company, they only have value to the buyer if they bring him some added advantages.

Thus the salesman should aim to sell security, profit, freedom from worry, efficiency, esteem and so on, because it is these pay-offs the buyer is looking for. The service itself is merely a means of meeting these ends.

Here is a list of services and products. If you were selling these, what would you 'sell' the buyer?

* Membership of a record club
* Luncheon vouchers
* A holiday in the West Country
* An evening class
* A personal pension scheme
* A career counselling service
* A library service
* Personal book-keeping
* A community health programme
* An office cleaning service

Exercise 4.2:   Features into benefits

We saw from Exercise 4.1 that it was possible to speculate about the various benefits which would be received by customers of a service. Sometimes it is possible to get confused over what is a benefit and what is a feature of the service. As we saw in Chapter 4 it is important to be able to recognize the difference between the two because ultimately it is benefits we sell. This exercise should help you to distinguish between features and benefits. Furthermore, it will help you to become very fluent in connecting one to the other.

Step 1

Cut some pieces of paper into twenty-four 'cards' of roughly playing card size. On eighteen of the cards write the following words or phrases which describe typical features: technical back-up; multinational company; long-established company; no intermediaries; range of services; reputation; technologically advanced; based on market research; training provided; market leader; not complicated; our experience; availability; flexible financial terms; family business; guarantees; fee/price; originality. Leave the remaining six cards blank for the time being.

Step 2

Study the cards you have made and decide if there are any other features you can think of which are not covered (think particularly of your own products and their features). As other features spring to mind, write each one down on the blank cards.

Step 3

Using the cards and any additional ones you have made as above, shuffle the pack of cards and place them face down in front of you.

Step 4

Turn over the top card, make a note of the feature it depicts and then respond to it by writing down a benefit that would arise from this feature. If this seems difficult, try using the phrase 'which means that' to connect the benefit to the feature. Repeat this procedure for the whole pack of cards.

Step 5

Turn to page 240 and check how your answers compare with the ones given there. If there is very much of a variance, it would be worthwhile for you to re-read Chapter 4.

Step 6

Now re-shuffle the pack and go through the exercise again, without referring to your earlier notes. This time list two benefits for each feature card. Again check your answers on page 240.
Note: This exercise is repeatable and so you ought to come back to it whenever you get a spare moment. The more fluent you become at associating benefits with features, the more effective you will be in sales situations.

Exercise 4.3: Benefit analysis of your own services

So far we have looked at services in general, except for the few features of your own particular service you might have added to the previous exercise. This exercise is designed to help you to apply the theory in Chapter 4 to your own special circumstances, using your own service as the learning vehicle.

Step 1

Remind yourself about what is involved in completing a benefit analysis sheet by studying the following form. If necessary, look back at Chapter 4 for an illustration of how a completed benefit analysis sheet might look (see pages 136–7).

Step 2

Using the blank benefit analysis sheet that follows complete it for a potentially major customer for your service.

Benefit analysis sheet

Customer: _____

Service(s) required: _____

Customer appeal	Features	Advantages	Benefits	Proof

Step 3

Make brief notes about how you will approach this potentially major customer, your opening statements and how you will introduce the major benefits to him.

Exercise 4.4: *Keep it simple*

In Chapter 4 it was stressed that communication between the salesman and the client ought to be kept as simple as possible by avoiding the use of complicated words or jargon. The following story illustrates the value of following this golden rule.

A plumber found that hydrochloric acid seemed to work very well for cleaning drains. However, not being certain if it was a permissible substance to use, he sought advice from the local authorities. This is an extract from the letter he received:

'. . . The efficiency of hydrochloric acid is indisputable, but the chlorine residue is incompatible with metallic permanence.'

The plumber wrote back to say he was pleased that they agreed with him that the acid worked well.

Alarmed, the local authority sent a second letter.

'. . . We cannot assume responsibility for the production of toxic or noxious residues with hydrochloric acid, and recommend that you use an alternative procedure.'

The plumber was not too sure what this meant so he checked. The third reply he understoood.

'. . . Don't use hydrochloric acid, it eats the hell out of drains.'

Sometimes there is no other word or phrase you can use if you are talking about a technical subject. But generally you will be able to find common words which will enable you to communicate more effectively. Work through this exercise and see if it is possible to reduce unnecessary blockages to good communications.

Step 1

Using the left-hand column of Worksheet 1 (page 148) make a list of all the 'jargon' words that are typically used in your service industry. Remember to include abbreviations and initials, they too are often the source of confusion. When you are satisfied you have collected a list of most of the jargon, move to Step 2.

Step 2

Using the right-hand column on the worksheet, against each jargon word or phrase, write down a simpler way it might be expressed.

Step 3

If there are some words where there really is no adequate substitution for the jargon, then underline them or highlight them in some way. Make a mental note to try to keep the use of these words to a minimum.

Note: Although this exercise has been developed in the context of face-to-face communication, clearly a similar reduction of jargon in letters or reports will improve their effectiveness also.

Worksheet 1: Keep it simple

Write down all the jargon words or phrases you typically use	Write down a simplified way of expressing what you have written in the left-hand column

5

Dealing with Objections

Overview

It is unrealistic for the salesman to expect to get through the sales interview without the buyer raising an objection. Whenever an objection is raised, it has to be answered, otherwise the salesman will be unable to progress to closing the sale.

If a buyer cannot see a need for the service on offer he will raise a fundamental objection. The salesman then has to work to demonstrate to the buyer that a need does in fact exist.

When a buyer does recognize a need for the service but delays making the decision to purchase or requires further convincing, then he is said to be raising a standard objection.

The best way for a salesman to deal with an objection is not to let it get raised by the buyer in the first place. Once he has stated his beliefs about the service or the offer, the buyer will be more entrenched in his position.

By using an objections analysis process the salesman can identify the main objections he can expect, categorize them and plan ways to forestall them or answer them. Underlying this type of analysis is the requirement for the salesman to understand why objections are raised and the best techniques for dealing with different types of objections.

Sometimes the buyer's objection is hidden from the salesman yet still prevents the interview from progressing to a close. By asking an incomplete question the salesman can often discover the nature of the hidden objection and, once out into the open, it can be dealt with.

The price objection is very common and yet many salesmen find it difficult to overcome. Their success rate improves considerably if they talk in terms of value rather than cost.

Discounts can be a negotiating tool for the salesman and help him to overcome the price objection, but often the negotiating value is given away too quickly by the salesman who doesn't work at answering the price objection in value terms.

A sale is never completed until the customer's money is in the bank. Therefore, especially in times of recession, the salesman must guard against doing business with inappropriate companies. Bad debts and late payment can combine to erode any profits the salesman might otherwise generate.

Dealing with objections

In working through the selling process, we have looked at how important it is for the salesman to prepare carefully for each interview he has with a buyer. We have discussed also the various ways he can open his meeting and how some openings will arrest the buyer's *attention* better than others.

The preceding chapter dealt with the theory and practice of benefit selling, the second part of our mnemonic A. B. C. Logically then, this chapter ought now to proceed to cover the final step, *closing* the sale.

It doesn't . . . and the reasons why will not have escaped discerning readers. Useful though A. B. C. is as a memory jogger and framework to the sales interview, things will not always run as smoothly as the formula suggests. Almost certainly, at some stage or another the buyer will raise objections.

It is easy to imagine what typical objections might be, for we have all used them from time to time when somebody has tried to sell us something.

'I don't like the colours.'
'It is too expensive.'
'It's not really what I am looking for.'
'I would like to go away and think about it.'
'We already have one.'
'I am not ready to take delivery yet.'
'I am not too happy about your guarantee.'
'I am not prepared to wait that long for it.'

To be successful the salesman must be able to overcome such objections before he can move to close the sale. If he fails to respond to them satisfactorily, then all of his careful planning and preparation will have been in vain.

Objections are natural

A buyer might raise an objection for a whole variety of reasons. It is only natural that he would do so, because if he is going to commit his own or his company's money to the purchase of a service, he has to be completely sure in his own mind that he is doing the right thing.

In fact, although an objection is at first sight an obstacle to closing the sale, on closer examination it can provide the salesman with some useful insights into the buyer's thinking and motivation.

Thus the salesman has to learn how to analyse the buyer's objection if he is to overcome it, or indeed use it to his advantage.

In practical terms, objections can be divided into two groups, fundamental objections and standard objections.

Fundamental objections

If the buyer fails to see the need for the service on offer, he will raise a fundamental objection. Perhaps the most typical example of this would be:

'We have no need for this service.'

In effect he is saying that neither your company nor your competitors are in a position to do business with him; a major stumbling block indeed.

Many salesmen when faced with such an objection will mutter apologies for taking up the buyer's time and head for the door. However, this doesn't have to be the case, as we shall discover later in this chapter.

Standard objections

A standard objection is used when the buyer recognizes his need for the service but wishes to delay making a decision in the salesman's favour. Such an objection might be rooted in natural caution, where perhaps the buyer just needs further convincing before he will conclude the deal.

Often further information or supporting evidence is enough to overcome this type of objection.

Other standard objections can be more difficult to cope with. Although the need is still there, the buyer perceives a major obstacle in the way, one that will require more than just information if it is to be cleared.

Dealing with objections

The best way of dealing with objections is deceptively simple – do not give the buyer the need to raise them in the first place.

Whenever a buyer raises an objection the salesman in effect has to prove him wrong if there is going to be movement towards a successful close. This has to be done politely, courteously and in such a way that it never develops into an argument or that the buyer feels annoyed or diminished by the outcome.

How much better, therefore, if the salesman were to identify before the meeting the likely objections which might be raised. He could then plan how to forestall them in his presentation and offer before they are voiced.

It is curious, but true, that once a person has actually said something, like voicing an objection, this verbal 'nailing of colours to the mast' makes it much more difficult to get him to shift his position afterwards.

Thus the salesman should try to develop his argument for buying the service in such a way that he is providing the buyer with a 'yessable' proposition at all stages of the interview and leaving no room for the objection.

But plan as he might, it will be impossible to anticipate every objection. The salesman must therefore learn techniques to deal with those objections that escaped detection at his preparation stage.

Dealing with fundamental objections

As we have seen, the buyer will raise this type of objection when he cannot see a need for the service on offer. In these circumstances benefit selling is clearly inappropriate and in fact will probably antagonize the buyer if it is attempted.

Since the buyer cannot see the need, the salesman will have to devote his efforts to convincing him that he actually does have a need, even if he hadn't recognized this to be the case.

As with examples provided elsewhere in this book, it is impossible to provide a 'magic' formula of words that will cover every situation. Nevertheless the following illustration shows how a salesman can work creatively and help the buyer to see a need which had previously not been apparent to him.

Example

Suppose the salesman is selling a private health insurance. The need for such schemes is not fully accepted by many people who believe in the concept of a National Health Service. Indeed the whole issue of medical treatment is not only political but is also highly-charged in emotional terms.

While some objections to a private health insurance scheme might be value judgments, it is still probable that many potential buyers would be unaware of how such a scheme operated in practice.

Thus the fundamental objection could be anticipated as 'I have no need for any sort of private health scheme', and the salesman blithely extolling the benefits of his particular scheme is doomed to failure, until he establishes a need.

The salesman should instead open the interview in such a way as to forestall this fundamental objection. For example:

'Mr Buyer, until recently many of our customers would never have dreamed of investing in a private health scheme. Now so many things seem to have changed. People are beginning to think that unless they do something about it themselves they are destined to have second-class medical treatment for themselves and their families.

'It surely can't be right that you should have to wait so long for minor operations or treatment. After all, it's so difficult to be at your best when you are not 100 per cent fit and the pressure at work never reduces, does it? And how can you plan ahead?

'Just look at the letters we have had from people like yourself who are now so relieved that they are doing the best for their family and safeguarding their work position.'

An opening like this may well make the buyer aware that there are perhaps good reasons for such a scheme that he had not considered earlier. He will realize that if he continues to ignore change he could be letting others down and conclude that it will probably be in his own interest to hear more about these schemes.

By selling the need at an early stage, the salesman forestalled the objection. This means that the salesman must always provide compelling reasons if he is to change the buyer's mind about his needs. He is well aware that once aired, the fundamental objection is doubly difficult to counter.

There will always be times when the objection really is fundamental. When faced with this, the salesman ought to change the subject and talk about another service with no obvious connection to the 'blocked' one. Alternatively he might cut his losses, admit that he misread the situation and then move on to his next call.

Dealing with standard objections

Whereas the salesman can expect to encounter fundamental objections when he is attempting to open business with new customers or when he is promoting a new service, the majority of objections he faces will be what we call standard objections.

They arise from the service itself or the offer. They surface in a number of guises best described as:
— feature objections, e.g. 'It is too big';
— lack of knowledge objections, e.g. 'It will be too complicated for us';
— delay objections, e.g. 'We will have to think this over';
— hidden objections, e.g. the buyer is hesitant to close;
— loyalty objections, e.g. 'Our present supplier is so good';
— price objections, e.g. 'It's too expensive'.

The salesman needs to understand why these objections are raised and to recognize their significance. Once he can do this, he is able to react accordingly, as we will show later.

The salesman never wants to get into an argument with the buyer. Therefore as a general rule the *apparent agreement* technique can be useful to avoid direct confrontation. It works like this:

Buyer: 'It is extremely expensive.'
Salesman: '*Yes* it is expensive Mr Buyer, *but* because it lasts twice as long as the best of the others, over the year you have in fact made significant savings. That is what you are looking for isn't it?'

This technique of agreeing (*yes*) demonstrates that the salesman understands the buyer's way of thinking, yet at the same time (*but*), is prepared to put another point of view.

Just think what the outcome might have been if the salesman responded to the buyer above differently:

Salesman: 'Oh! No it isn't!'

It doesn't bear thinking about, does it?

Let us now look in more detail at the different ways the salesman can deal with the various types of standard objections.

Feature objections

If the buyer is unhappy about a particular feature of the service, he will raise an objection about it. Many objections result in this way, which is unfortunate because on the whole they are largely avoidable.

In the previous chapter we looked at benefit analysis and saw that the various benefits had to be reviewed in the light of their customer appeal.

Well, a parallel technique can be used to forestall the feature objection. This time, instead of listing benefits, features are used and rated for their customer appeal. Then, as the offer is proposed, those features with maximum customer appeal are stressed.

The prudent salesman will also prepare his responses to the other feature objections, knowing that from time to time they too are raised. An example of an objection analysis sheet is given on page 157.

Forestalling a feature objection

Here is an example of a salesman forestalling a feature objection. Imagine that he represents a company that offers an office equipment rental service. He knows that one common feature

Objections analysis sheet for ....(Type of service)

Most common objections (Typical words that are used)	The type of objection (e.g. Feature, price)	Ways to forestall objections (Try writing what you would say)	Ways to answer objections (Write what you would say)

Figure 10 *An objections analysis sheet*

Note: Remember the impact of customer appeal in your replies objection is that their equipment tends to be at the larger, more sophisticated end of the range, while buyers are often looking for more modest machinery. He might forestall the buyer's objection as follows:

> 'Mr Buyer, one of the main advantages of this particular photocopier is that it is capable of handling high workloads without undue strain. It's rather like when you have a car with a larger engine; it doesn't labour so much when you have to put your foot down. This means that our machine can churn out work, day after day, while smaller machines keep needing maintenance . . . and generally at the most inconvenient times. You wouldn't want to find yourself suddenly without a photocopier, would you Mr Buyer?'

This approach has several things to commend it:
- it turns what the buyer may have seen as a disadvantage into an advantage;
- by ending with a question, the salesman invites a positive response from the buyer which, as we have discussed before, will commit the buyer in favour of this feature;
- the buyer's objection is forestalled in a business-like manner which is likely to enhance the salesman's credibility.

Answering a feature objection

Suppose on this particular occasion the salesman had not thought to forestall the buyer's objection. He is now faced with overcoming the objection, 'This photocopier really seems too big for what we had in mind.'

Here is a ready-made situation for the salesman to use a technique which gives the impression of agreeing with the buyer, but which still enables the objections to be overcome.

> 'Yes Mr Buyer, I can quite see your point, *but* we have found that this size machine is so much more reliable than smaller models. After all, none of our customers would want to feel their

photocopier might keep breaking down. It doesn't help their business and it does very little for our reputation. Surely it is not a risk worth taking, is it Mr Buyer?'

Again, the question at the end obtains a response from the buyer which will confirm that he has 'talked himself' out of the objection.

Information seeking objections

While at first sight these might look similar to feature objections, closer study shows them to be rooted in the customer's lack of knowledge or understanding about the service or offer.

It is this information gap which causes the buyer to object to the offer, on the grounds that he or his organization will not be properly served if the purchase went ahead.

Often the buyer is unaware of the information gap, but intuitively senses that something is not quite right with the offer. This is what he might say:

'It seems very complicated. I don't think our staff would be capable of operating it.'

'It sounds a first-rate service, but I couldn't possibly find the money to pay for it.'

Such objections are to be welcomed by the salesman because in each case they imply that the buyer is interested in the offer, but still sees a drawback.

All the salesman has to do in these circumstances is to demonstrate that the objections really have no substance. If he can do this, he is virtually at a stage where he can close.

Let us consider how the salesman might respond to the above objections: the too-complicated objection – 'But suppose we arranged to train your staff, would you go ahead then?'; the can't find the money objection – 'but suppose I arranged easy terms for you. Would you go ahead then?'

The phrase 'but suppose' is very useful in these situations because it tests whether or not the objection is real. Moreover it does this in a way that is not at all challenging to the buyer.

The question at the end, 'Would you go ahead then?' is again used to get a positive response and hence commitment from the buyer.

Delay objections

'Well, you will realize that I now have to talk it over with my colleagues.'

'I need time to think about this. Can you come back in a couple of weeks' time?'

These are typical examples of the delay objection. They are particularly difficult for the salesman to deal with because in many ways these objections sound to be so reasonable. None of us like to be rushed into making a decision.

The big problem for the salesman is to establish whether or not the buyer is avoiding making a decision for reasons other than he states. It is imperative that the salesman discovers if the delay is 'genuine', otherwise he might return later to find that the business has gone to a competitor.

In fact there are three possibilities for the delay objection being used:
— the buyer is not really convinced;
— he genuinely needs time to consult or reflect;
— there is some other reason for avoiding the decision.

Buyer not convinced

If this happens, it means that the salesman has not proved his case. Somewhere, somehow, his sales offer was incomplete. After all, if the buyer had been convinced there would have been no reason to delay. Decisions are not like some wines, they rarely improve with age. If the salesman's case was right, then it will be just as right today as it would be in a week's time.

Faced with an unconvinced buyer the salesman may have to go over the main points a second time. For example:

> 'Well Mr Buyer, let us just check that we have covered everything . . . (covers all main points). It certainly seems that our service meets all your requirements, doesn't it?'

Extra time needed

If extra time is genuinely required, the buyer will have hinted at the fact earlier in the discussion: 'At the moment I am only conducting a feasibility study. We are not entirely certain if we want to diversify into this field yet.' This is where the salesman who really *listens* scores over his contemporaries.

Similarly, if other people are involved in the decision-making process (remember the D.M.U. from Chapter 1?), then as likely as not, the salesman will have prepared for this. He can turn the delay objection to his advantage.

> 'Could I speak to your colleagues Mr Buyer? I'm sure that between us we will be able to answer all their queries.'

> 'How would you like me to arrange a demonstration for your colleagues?'

> 'Perhaps it would be helpful if I made a presentation to your board of directors.'

This technique has the merit of not only offering help or support to the buyer, but also it ensures that the 'undiluted' case is put forward by the salesman himself and does not ultimately depend upon the capabilities of a less knowledgeable person.

Other reasons

If the sales offer has been complete and there does not appear to be
any reason for delaying the purchase decision, then there must be
something still blocking the purchase which the buyer has chosen
not to disclose. These blocks are called hidden objections.

Hidden objections

The salesman is only human and in fairness could be expected to
overcome only those objections of which he is aware. Therefore, if
in spite of all his efforts, his customer claims to have all the
information he needs yet still prevaricates, it has to be assumed
there is an unanswered objection, hidden from the salesman.

The only prospect of making any progress from this point is for
the salesman to attempt to get this hidden objection out into the
open.

An effective technique for doing this is to invite the buyer to
complete an unfinished sentence. The power behind this technique
is that it appears to the buyer that the salesman has already guessed
at this yet unexpressed objection. When unexpectedly asked to give
voice, the buyer will often oblige and the truth emerges.

This is how the salesman does it:

'It seems then that price isn't a problem Mr Buyer, so *your
reason for not deciding is?*'

The words in italics are the key phrase when this technique is
used.

The salesman should concentrate closely on the buyer when he
asks the question and it is important to end in mid-sentence. A
pause might follow, but this should not be broken by the salesman.
The silence is a measure of the buyer's thought processes. Eventually two possible outcomes can be expected:

1 The buyer says that he didn't have any other reasons, to which the salesman confesses that he thought the buyer had mentioned something else. He then moves on to the close.

2 The buyer cannot avoid giving a truthful answer to the incomplete sentence, which gives the salesman an opportunity to overcome the objection then move towards the close.

The success of this technique lies in the key phrase '... so your reason for not deciding is?'. It is impossible to answer this without volunteering some useful information.

Just look what happens when a different formula of words is used, such as:

'Is there some reason you haven't mentioned for you not making a decision now?'

This almost invites a 'no' response and the salesman finishes up being none the wiser about the hidden objection.

Loyalty objections

The loyalty objection is often met by salesmen making their first call. It is most common when the service is a regular one which has caused a relationship to be built up between the supplier and the buying company.

'We deal with all our insurance matters through our local broker. He has been most helpful over the years.'

'We were one of Acme's first customers and they look after us very well. We don't see any reason to change.'

Perhaps 'loyalty' is a misnomer, although undoubtedly it does play a part. What we actually see here are expressions of confidence that the buyers have in their suppliers.

We all know that confidence isn't won easily and this is why 'loyalty' objections are so difficult for the salesman to overcome.

The offer of keener prices, better service or newer technology from a new and untried supplier are not always enough to tip the balance in the salesman's favour when weighed against confidence built up over the years with existing suppliers.

Nevertheless, being faced with such a situation is one of the challenges of a salesman's life. Indeed it should be seen in this light, rather than a hopeless cause, because the salesman will need all the enthusiasm he can muster if he is to overcome the loyalty objection.

From the outset, things might not be as black as they seem. Established suppliers are known to take long-standing customers for granted. They stop providing the service calls they used to give, business becomes routine and their salesmen become too casual or over-confident.

Often factors like these can work to the new salesman's advantage once he refuses to accept the situation on its face value.

When faced with the loyalty objection the salesman should:

1 Persist, be enthusiastic and work to develop buyer confidence.
2 Always have a good reason for calling on the customer, perhaps to explain a new benefit, the application of new technology or a success story from a similar customer.
3 Develop reasons for the buyer to change his current supply provisions. For example, shouldn't he safeguard his interest by having a second supplier instead of always relying on the one?
4 Never 'knock' the opposition. This is tantamount to saying that the buyer has poor judgment. It is better to be complimentary about his existing suppliers and then use the opportunity to stress a differential benefit. For example:

> '*Yes*, the software they produce is very good, but do you know we now supply all the leading computer manufacturers with their software packages.'

Note that our old friends *yes* and *but* can again be useful in these circumstances.

Sooner or later, the persistent and enthusiastic salesman will make a breakthrough and get the business he seeks.

The fatal traps to avoid are for him to:
– give up too readily;
– use 'anything for me today' types of approaches.

Price objections

Since most buyers see their jobs as buying in the services their company needs at the lowest possible price, it should come as no surprise that price objections figure prominently in many sales interviews.

For many buyers, raising a price objection has become a standard ploy that they use in their attempt to bargain for a lower price.

In reality, however, the buyer is more likely to be concerned with value for money. As we saw in Chapter 1, the buyer is not always the free agent he might pretend to be. Invariably he will need to justify his decisions to others and his vocabulary for doing so will be 'reliability', 'quality', 'long term savings', and so on.

The price objection, like any other, must therefore be answered by benefits which emphasize value in terms of customer appeal. Moreover, value must be clearly explained and illustrated in terms that the customer can understand and accept. Only then will he be prepared to agree that the additional cost is justified.

Here are some areas where 'value' can be established.

1 *Efficiency* – the performance of the service compared with alternatives.
2 *Economy* – savings in labour, time, cost and so on due to superior features of the service on offer.
3 *Service* – ways in which back-up or after-sales service is superior to rival suppliers, e.g. delivery, installation, technical advice, guarantees, training, trade-in arrangements, maintenance contracts, etc.

If the salesman has confidence in the service he offers then he should never be afraid of the price objection. He will always be able to prove to the buyer that the benefits package he provides is worth the additional cost.

Ways to diminish the price objection

While it might not be possible to completely forestall the price objection, it is certainly possible to reduce the emphasis on price in the buyer's mind. Here are some techniques for doing this.

1 *'It only costs . . .'* – use of the word *'only'* implies that the service cost is low compared with the competition or all the benefits it provides.
2 *Focus on price difference rather than the actual price* – usually price differences are not all that great for similar services. Therefore the salesman should keep stressing the difference in price and all the differential benefits that accrue to the buyer.

> 'Mr Buyer, it is true that we are talking of a service that costs £1,500 and you could buy something similar for £1,300. But let us just think for a moment about what you get for that extra £200. First there is . . .'

3 *Talk about minimized figures* – for example, a management training course for 10 people might be quoted at £4,000. It would be equally true, and perhaps less disturbing, to talk about it in terms of 'only £400 per person, which is very reasonable'.
 Similarly, fees might be broken down and presented as a daily rate of, for example, £200, rather than emphasizing that the whole project will cost £100,000.

When to start talking about price

Ideally the salesman will want to forestall a price objection with a good sales offer. Once he has had the opportunity to explain all the benefits, it becomes easier to justify the cost.

However, if the buyer raises the question of price before the sales offer is complete, the salesman must never refuse to give it. To avoid answering will make it look as if the salesman has something to hide, which implies that the price must be high.

If the salesman, in truth, cannot give the price because he needs more information, then he should say so.

'Mr Buyer, the price will depend on how we finalize the arrangements and how many times you expect to use our services. Should we move on to discuss these matters now?'

Discounts

Many companies give the salesman some leeway in the prices he can charge for the service. They recognize that price objections exist and trust that by giving the salesman the authority to negotiate a discount, all will be well.

Sensible though this sounds, in practice too many salesmen, when faced with a price objection, immediately give away their discretionary discount. They barely attempt to overcome the objection in the way we have discussed, instead they capitulate and denude themselves of any negotiating power.

The outcome from all of this is that the company have in effect reduced their prices in return for no extra business.

This whole subject of discretionary discounts for salesmen is one which exercises many companies today. Clearly, it is an area which has to be planned and managed very carefully.

Credit-worthiness

There is always much pressure on salesmen to 'go out and get business'. In times of recession this pressure becomes even more intense as long-established customers cut back on their orders and rival salesmen strive to maintain their previous levels of growth at your expense.

In their effort to reach their sales quota some salesmen are prepared to conduct business with customers who are not financially sound. Certainly, it gets their sales manager off their back for a few days, but in the longer term it is a disaster for their company.

Bad debts and the interest lost on overdue accounts can steadily erode all the profit they thought they were generating when the order was taken.

Salesmen must understand that a sale is not complete until the money from the customer is banked.

Summary

1   *Listen to what the buyer is saying and do not interrupt*

Let the buyer give his objection in full and never attempt to stop him, even if you know what is coming next. Pay him the courtesy of really listening to what he has to say and try to give responsive, intelligent replies rather than slick, well-rehearsed answers.

No buyer is impressed with the over-clever salesman.

Unless the salesman appears to be interested in the buyer and his problems, he will never win the buyer's confidence.

2   *Appear to agree*

'*Yes* I can appreciate your concern, *but* have you. . . .'

3   *Back up answers with proof*

Just as benefits need to be backed up, so do answers to objections. Plan ahead about what proof might be required.

4   *Never argue*

The salesman's job is to build confidence and trust, not conflict.

5   Question the objection

The salesman needs to know if the objection is real or game playing. The 'but suppose' technique is a useful test in these situations.

6   *The objection must be answered if it is real*

And if it is hidden the salesman must try to get it into the open by using the unfinished question 'and your other reason for not deciding is . . . ?'

Application questions

1 Select one of your company's services. Give examples of fundamental objections, feature objections and information seeking objections to it. Do the latter two objections provide feedback for potential design improvements or revised sales literature?

2 Make a list of all the various 'proofs' you can use to back up the claims of your sales offer. Which of these seem to be the most powerful in terms of impact on customers? What does this tell you about customer needs?

3 When you are negotiating with a buyer, what type of buyer behaviour do you find most difficult to handle? What technique have you developed to help you cope with this type of buyer?

Exercises

Exercise 5.1:   Objection analysis 1

We all know that it would be unrealistic to expect to go through a sales interview without the client raising one or two objections about our proposition. The first exercise is designed to help you

Worksheet 1: Objection analysis

Prepare a list of the objections most commonly raised by your customers about a specific service you offer. Against each objection make a note about the way you usually respond to it.

Most common objection	My usual response

recall the most common objections you experience in your day-to-day work and to record how you respond to them at present. From this starting point we will proceed to examine if there might be better ways to answer objections, but for now, follow the instructions on Worksheet 1 (page 170).

Exercise 5.2:   Objection analysis 2

Having listed the most common objections you experience in your work (Worksheet 1), we will now proceed to analyse them using the technique described in Chapter 5 and see how they might be forestalled and countered.

For the moment, try to put your usual responses to the back of your mind and react to each objection in the way this analysis technique leads you. This is not to suggest that your usual responses are necessarily wrong, but to go into this exercise with preconceived notions will clearly reduce the chances of developing any new ideas.

Step 1

Refer back to Chapter 5 and recap on the section about objection analysis. Using Worksheet 2 (page 173) enter the name or description of the particular service under consideration at the top of the page.

Step 2

Transfer the 'most common objections' listed on Worksheet 1 to the left-hand column of Worksheet 2.

Step 3

Analyse each objection in turn and identify its nature e.g. feature, price, fundamental, hidden, etc. Write your decision in the second column on Worksheet 2.

Step 4

Taking the most common objection at the top of your list (which you have now categorized into an objection type) write down the words you would use to forestall the client raising this objection. Enter your response or responses in the third column of the worksheet. Continue across the page into the next column and write down how you would now respond to this objection if it were raised. Again more than one response is permissible.

Step 5

Repeat Step 4 for all the remaining objections listed on Worksheet 2. Use separate sheets of notepaper if the printed worksheet is not large enough for your needs.

Step 6

When you have finished Worksheet 2, look back on what you have written. In those cases where you have listed more than one response in the 'forestalling' or 'answer' columns, underline the response that you think will be the most effective. These clearly will become useful 'tools' in future sales interviews.

Step 7

Finally check back with Worksheet 1 and see if the ways that you would now answer the most common objections differ from the way you had been answering them in the past. Make any notes that will remind you of useful points that emerged from this exercise and will help you in the future.

Exercise 5.3:   Dealing with objections

This exercise is designed to consolidate on the work from Exercises

Worksheet 2: Objection analysis 2

Objections analysis sheet for . . . (type of service)

Most common objections (typical words that are used)	The type of objection e.g. feature, price	Ways to forestall objection (try writing what you would say)	Ways to answer objection (write what you would say)

Note: Remember the impact of customer appeal in your replies

5.1 and 5.2. Valuable though it is to be able to prepare an objections analysis in advance, we can never be a 100 per cent certain how the client will react to our sales proposition. Therefore we have to develop the mental agility to be able to respond to almost any objection in a confident and winning manner. This exercise should help you to develop the skill to do this.

Step 1

Cut some pieces of paper into twenty 'cards' of roughly playing card size. On fifteen of the cards write the following phrases which describe typical objections: 'It's too expensive'; 'I'm not prepared to wait that long'; 'It isn't quite what I'm looking for'; 'We've had bad experiences with your company'; 'There must be a catch somewhere'; 'Your literature is difficult to understand'; 'Your guarantee is less than your competitor's'; 'I haven't heard of your company before'; 'You are too small to help us'; 'It will be too complicated for our staff'; 'You keep sending different people to see me'; 'We are not like your other customers'; 'We are happy with our existing supplier'; 'We only buy British'; 'We have our own experts'. Leave the remaining five cards blank for the time being.

Step 2

Carefully study the cards you have made and make a note of any typical objections that you often encounter which are not listed on these cards. Write these objections on the blank cards, using a separate card for each objection.

Step 3

Shuffle the pack of cards and lay them face down in front of you.

Step 4

Turn over the top card, make a note of the objection and then write down how you would respond.

Step 5

Repeat this process until you have worked your way through the whole pack of cards. Now turn to page 245 and check your answers.

Note: This exercise can be repeated from time to time as you work through the study programme, thereby improving your fluency at overcoming objections.

Exercise 5.4: *The missed sale*

We have looked at dealing with objections in some detail in the previous exercises. In the case study which follows did Brian Hopcraft the salesman fail to overcome an objection? If so, what was the nature of the objection? Or was he just unlucky? Read the story about the missed sale and make notes about what the salesman might have done differently. After you have made your notes, check on page 247 to see how they compare with ours.

Stanley Broderick was a 'proud' man and took his responsibilities as his family's breadwinner very seriously. He was now more or less over the shock of being made redundant after eighteen years loyal service in the tool design department of a leading British company.

His redundancy payment had cushioned him to some extent and now he was beginning a new career as a self-employed tool design consultant. His contacts in industry were numerous and the early results of his new business looked promising. However, his natural caution ensured that he didn't get carried away by his success, after all, Stanley recognized that he was faced with a still uncertain future.

His immediate problem was to get life cover insurance to replace the cover he had automatically received as an employee with his previous company. He wasn't too sure how much he could afford to pay because he found it difficult to predict how much he would consistently earn.

He hadn't confided these doubts about his future earnings to his wife because he had not wanted to worry her. Jane Broderick was a worrier by nature and in many ways had been hit harder by Stanley's redundancy than he himself.

To shelter Jane, Stanley continually stressed his new contacts and promises of fruitful contracts just around the corner. As a result, she was beginning to see the vision of a future that would be very rosy indeed.

The Brodericks were waiting at home for Brian Hopcraft, an insurance consultant, to visit them.

Hopcraft drove away from the Brodericks puzzled that he hadn't made a sale. After all, by his book he had done everything right.

As he made his way home he reflected on the evening's visit. . . .

Brian Hopcraft's experienced eye had quickly assessed the earnings level of someone who could afford to live in such a desirable property as the Brodericks. A much sought after locality too. Already he was thinking of suitable life cover policies.

Nothing happened to change his mind when the carved oak door of the newly built porch extension was opened by Broderick and he was admitted into an impressively furnished hall.

The children of the house, it transpired, were out at a youth club and so Broderick had ushered Hopcraft into the lounge to conduct their business.

On entering the room he had made his introductions to Mrs Broderick, while mentally making a confirming appraisal of the surroundings. Hopcraft had insisted that Mrs Broderick remained, even though she had offered to leave the two men alone to talk business. He knew from experience that she would be an ally; didn't the wife always say a little bit more than the husband? His hunch was proved to be correct.

He had asked all the usual questions and made a convincing sales offer for an attractive, if expensive, life cover policy with profits. It clearly matched up with the needs of the Brodericks, as Jane Broderick was quick to appreciate. Yet, for some reason, Stanley had remained strangely reticent.

Hopcraft thought back about the way he had summarized the main points of the offer – the outstanding mortgage, the children's continuing education, loss of expected earnings, upkeep of the house and so on – yes, it had seemed just right.

But he failed to close the sale. Broderick insisted that he needed time to think it over and eventually Hopcraft had to agree with this outcome.

Where could he have possibly gone wrong?

Exercise 5.5: *Analysis of negotiating style*

This exercise is designed to help you to analyse your 'negotiating' style when you deal with clients and, having analysed it, make decisions about:

1 How effective it is.
2 In what ways you might (if required) develop a more effective style.

Instructions

1 Study the statements made on the following pages and score them as follows. For example, in Section 1, if you thought that Statement C was most descriptive of your planning skills, then you would record this as your first choice on Worksheet 3, the Results Form (page 182). Now select the second most descriptive statement and designate this as your second choice on the Results Form. Record how each of the other statements describes your planning skills. Clearly the least descriptive becomes your fifth choice.

Note: You are not allowed to allocate half points or to have dead heats.

2 Work through the remaining sections in a similar way, entering all your choices on the Results Form, Worksheet 3.

3 Transfer the results from Worksheet 3 to Worksheet 4 (page 182) and obtain figures for the total scores (right-hand column).

4 Turn to page 248 to interpret what these scores mean.

Section 1 – Planning skills

A   I prepare my agenda well enough to achieve a good level of success at negotiating without too many problems. I always find that working to an orderly routine helps to ease the pressure on both sides.

B   I formulate my plans well in advance, and do my best to avoid any deviations. By having my programme well organized, the negotiating time is used to maximum advantage, and fewer objections are likely to be raised.

C   Although my plans are made well in advance, they have to be flexible. I must be able to adjust my programme to take account of the needs of the other party, since I am sure that they would do the same for me.

D   During any negotiation, new ideas keep coming from both sides all the time. Because of this, I find little advantage in planning my moves in too much detail or too far in advance. I prefer to 'play it by ear'.

E   I put effort into planning in terms of ultimate objectives. I assess all relevant information in advance and try to see both sides of the issue to anticipate possible difficulties.

Section 2 – Personal integrity

A   I believe that integrity on both sides leads to a successful outcome. I readily admit when I am uncertain of any factor. My aim is to give the other party a set of expectations on which he can rely.

B   Sometimes I have to bend the truth a little in order to get a favourable decision. Since I have the utmost faith in my company and product, I believe that this is justified. In the long run, results are all that count.

C   I find that the best way to preserve my integrity is to make as few commitments as possible and only make promises which are well within my capability to perform. Any other course of action will only lead to trouble later on.

D   I always approach a negotiation with optimism and concentrate on the positive advantages which I can offer the customer. In order to achieve mutual satisfaction, I sometimes have to gloss over the negative points.

E   It is important to keep to the strict truth in a negotiation and I never say anything which cannot be supported with facts. Sometimes the other side may misinterpret what has been said but no blame can be attached to anyone who keeps to factual data.

Section 3 – Attitude to power

A   Both sides in negotiation must accept the strong and the weak points of the other. It is legitimate for either party to exploit their power, but working to solve each other's problems, both gain power together.

B   The ideal negotiating situation occurs when power is equally balanced. I find that it is then much easier to achieve a working relationship where both sides can attain reasonable objectives.

C   Power should be exercised carefully in negotiation. I sometimes find it better to play down my strong points to avoid unnecessary conflict. It is possible to win points without antagonising the other party.

D   When I am in a strong position, I do my best to exploit it to the full. Conversely, I am at pains never to reveal a weak base;

when a point is made strongly enough, the other side will usually back down.

E   When my opponent is in a strong position, I try to avoid any bargaining situations. In negotiation it is best not to expect too much – because if one side gets more, the other side is bound to get less.

Section 4 – Reaction to stress

A   I try to remain detached during negotiation and avoid making controversial statements or claims. In this way, I rarely find myself stressed by annoying or irritating situations.

B   I have always found that stressful situations can be resolved by warm and friendly understanding. The most important aim should be to keep the relationship together.

C   It is difficult to negotiate efficiently when under any form of tension. I therefore try to be firm but fair and aim for a mutually acceptable solution.

D   When stress occurs, I try to identify the reasons and resolve the underlying causes. On other occasions, I usually manage to control my reactions, although I see no harm in showing some impatience at times.

E   A level of stress often arises during negotiations and I am always ready to defend my position. In case my views are not accepted, I always have alternative arguments prepared.

Section 5 – Handling objections

A   I believe that it is necessary to be able to respond to objections with strong arguments and facts about the service, because without these a sale will be lost.

B   I believe it is best to avoid unpleasantness during a sales negotiation. Therefore, unless an objection can be easily answered, I will switch to another aspect of the service which is less likely to sour the relationship between me and the customer.

C   Wherever possible, I try to avoid discussing objections. Because there is little I can personally do to make the service more effective, I find it pays to stay fairly non-committed.

D   I try to encourage the customer to be open with me about any misgivings he might have about the service. In this way I begin to understand what is really important for him and can identify if it is possible to do something to remove these real objections.

E   I find that when a customer raises an objection, instead of answering it directly, it pays to come up with some other features or benefits of the service that equal or surpass the drawbacks of the original objection. Sometimes it is possible to overcome an objection by giving the customer something extra, after all, business is all about 'give and take'.

Section 6 – Team leadership

A   I get together with the members of my team to plan our overall strategy. I assess their ideas and reactions and together we establish our main objectives and work out flexible tactics to meet them.

B   I explain the overall objectives in detail to my team and allocate responsibilities according to capabilities. I make sure that everyone is satisfied that he understands the part he has to play.

C   I encourage the other team members to discuss objectives with me. When they need my help I give the problem my fullest attention and offer whatever suggestions I can.

D   The other members of my team are all experts in their own fields. I give them all the basic facts they need and it would only cause confusion if I were to interfere too much in what they do.

E   As a teamleader, I set the objectives and decide the strategy. I always make certain that everyone in my team knows exactly what he has to do, as well as how and when to do it.

Worksheet 3:   Results form

Choice	Section 1 Planning skills	Section 2 Personal integrity	Section 3 Attitude to power	Section 4 Reaction to stress	Section 5 Handling objections	Section 6 Team leader- ship
1st						
2nd						
3rd						
4th						
5th						

Worksheet 4:   Style analysis form

Now transfer the information from Worksheet 3 to Worksheet 4 below in the following way. This is what happens. Your first choice in each section scores 5 points, your second choice scores 4 points, your third choice scores 3 points, your fourth choice scores 2 points and your fifth choice scores 1 point. For example, if your choice for Section 1 had been A, B, C, D, E, in that order, then Section 1 of your Worksheet 4 would look as follows:

Example

Section 1 Planning skills		Sect
E	1	
D	2	
B	4	
C	3	
A	5	

You can now transfer your scores for each section to the half squares in Worksheet 4 below. By adding the scores *across* the rows you will reach a total score for each negotiating style. Interpretation of the scores is explained in the Model Answer 5.5

Negotiating style	Section 1 Planning skills	Section 2 Personal integrity	Section 3 Attitude to power	Section 4 Reaction to stress	Section 5 Handling objections	Section 6 Team leader- ship	Score total
9:9	E	E	A	D	D	A	
5:5	D	D	B	C	E	B	
9:1	B	B	D	E	A	F.	
1:9	C	A	C	B	B	D	
1:1	A	C	E	A	C	C	

Note:

1 If there is a difference between the highest score and the second highest of 9 points or more, then it suggests that the preferred negotiating style (highest score) is quite fixed and it would be difficult to adopt a different style.

2 If the difference between each score is only in the order of 2 or 3 points, i.e., the whole range of score is encompassed by 10–12 points, then it suggests that there is no clear, overall preferred style. Irrespective of the actual highest style score, that person is said to be exhibiting a statistical 5:5 negotiating style and it should be regarded as 5:5.

6

Techniques for Closing the Sale

Overview

The sale is closed only when the buyer makes a firm commitment to place an order. But during the sales interview the buyer will often show interest, ask questions, or make committing statements, all of which are buying signals to the perceptive salesman.

Since there is a danger that buying signals could be misinterpreted, the salesman needs to ask questions to confirm that he is 'reading' the situation correctly.

The salesman should be constantly looking for opportunities to close the sale at any moment of the sales interview. To help him gauge if the time is right he will use trial closes to test the buyer's reactions and assess his level of interest.

Trial closes also help the salesman to retain the initiative during the interview and gradually accumulate a number of small commitments from the buyer which collectively can be used to close the sale.

The salesman should use direct and indirect questions to obtain buyer commitment. It is sometimes possible to lead the buyer into committing himself by offering him alternatives. As soon as he states a preference for one of these, it becomes relatively easy to follow with a close.

Other opportunities to close can be created by the summary technique, giving a quotation or by offering a concession.

In the final analysis, the salesman will only achieve a close if he *asks for an order*.

Techniques for closing the sale

So far in this book we have looked at the whole selling process with the exception of the 'C' of A.B.C. – the Close. In fact, all the preceding topics – understanding the buying process, preparing for the interview, obtaining the interview, opening techniques, benefit selling and dealing with objections – can now be seen in their true context, as steps towards the salesman's ultimate objective of closing the sale.

However, to close a sale successfully, the salesman needs to have a number of techniques at his disposal. In this chapter we will look at these techniques and consider the most appropriate circumstances in which to use them.

When is a sale closed?

Only when the buyer has committed himself by actually signing an order, submitting a written request for the service, or by providing an order number, can the sale be considered closed.

Promises that an order will be placed, or that the order will be available at the salesman's next visit, are not closes but merely prevarication on the part of the buyer.

Opportunities to close

As we have said, the whole sales interview should be seen as a process leading to a close. But this is not to say that the salesman has to go through the whole process before he can close the sale.

Clearly, if the buyer has carefully considered what he needs before the interview and has already weighed up the pros and cons of buying a particular service, the salesman will not have to sell benefits or overcome objections. He can make the sale virtually at the start of the meeting. (Indeed not to do so in these circumstances would probably work against the salesman's interests, because as we have seen earlier, doubts and uncertainties could start creeping into the buyer's mind the longer the interview progressed.)

Therefore throughout the interview the salesman has to be listening and watching for any signals that could indicate an opportunity to close.

More often than not, the salesman will have to complete his sales offer before he can close. The successful salesman, however, will know how to recognize buying signals, thereby saving time and effort in bringing the interview to a profitable conclusion.

Buying signals

Buying signals tend to originate when the buyer's interest is aroused. How the buyer then actually behaves can be observed in a number of different ways.

Body language

Most people convey with their 'body language' when they have become interested in a sales offer, for example when:
- the buyer who was looking bored and disinterested suddenly becomes animated;
- the buyer who was doodling as the salesman talked, stops and listens;
- the buyer who was leaning back in his chair, suddenly leans forward;
- the buyer voluntarily picks up literature or a sales proposal and begins to study it in detail;
- the buyer operates a demonstration model for a second or third time;
- the buyer keeps picking up a sample and examining it closely.

All these are signals that the buyer is interested, but the salesman must be certain that he is not misinterpreting the situation, because body language can be dangerously misleading at times.

He does this by asking a question designed to check that the buyer's new surge of interest was triggered by something the salesman said. Here are some examples:

> 'I get the feeling, Mr Buyer, that it is our after-sales service which is so important to you and sets us apart from our competitors?'

> 'Is it our early payments scheme that makes our proposal so attractive, Mr Buyer?'

An affirmative answer to such questions is almost an open invitation to close the sale.

Objections

Sometimes an objection can be a buying signal. This is especially true of 'information seeking' objections. Lack of information could be the one remaining barrier to the buyer being convinced about the sales offer.

Thus the salesman has to learn how to distinguish the genuine objection, when the buyer is obviously displaying a lot of interest in the offer, from the intellectual objection, which smacks of game playing and is used more to keep the buyer in control of the interview.

Committing statements or questions

Here are some typical examples that disclose the buyer's interest.

> 'It certainly sounds to be what I am looking for.'

> 'When we purchase this, you did say that we can renegotiate the contract after 12 months?'

Notice the way the word 'when' is used rather than 'if'. The buyer is already imagining he has purchased the service. This psychological 'ownership' of the service can show itself in other ways.

'I will be able to increase my private pension payments at a later stage, won't I?'

'. . . and you will guarantee to train our staff?'

When asked questions such as these the salesman should do two things:

1 Reassure the buyer
2 Ask a question

Here is a way the salesman could reply to the last question:

'Certainly Mr Buyer. We will train all your keyboard operators and in addition run a short appreciation course for your managers so that they will understand how our system works. That should ensure a smooth changeover, shouldn't it?'

The salesman's question at the end is most important because it enables him to check that he has interpreted the buying signal correctly.

Exactly how the salesman proceeds to follow up the buying signal will be covered later in this chapter.

Suppose there are no clear buying signals?

Even if the prospective buyer does not convey a positive buying signal, there eventually comes a point when he has a complete understanding of the proposition.

With a simple proposition this might occur at the first meeting. With a more complex sales offer it might take several meetings before this level of understanding is reached. Whichever of these happens to be the case, once this 'learning process' is completed, the buyer might of his own accord say that he wants to place an order. More typically, however, he will need to be prompted by the salesman.

How is this done? Quite simply, *the salesman asks for an order.* If the salesman hesitates to do this, then the buyer can take control of the situation by raising objections or delays. For example:

'That's fine, but I will need to consult my colleagues.'

As we have said before, promises will not do, because in the intervening time the buyer might change his mind or, as often happens, a competitor can step in to win the order.

Asking for the order

For the salesman this is the moment of truth. This is the reason that he spent all that time on research, planning, meeting people, demonstrating and preparing a persuasive sales offer.

Rather than risk receiving 'no' as an answer, many salesmen prefer to spin out their relationship with the buyer. To them a vague promise of an order sometime in the future is preferable to facing up to the defeat that 'no' brings with it.

For this reason, the fear of being rejected, the average salesman rarely asks for an order. And yet, paradoxically, experience shows that many buyers will not place an order unless they are actually *asked* to do so.

The salesman must therefore at the appropriate moment ask for the order. If he cannot leave with this, then he must secure an order number or some other positive commitment from the customer such as a deposit against the purchase.

Different closing techniques

As we have said, the buyer often needs to be prompted by the salesman. Even though the buyer might have been giving a number of buying signals, he will still need a gentle push to help him eventually to make up his mind.

There are a number of different closing techniques which enable the salesman to give the required impetus.

Trial closes

The timing of the close is extremely critical. Try to close too soon and the buyer will feel pressurized and become defensive. Leave it too late, and the buyer might start thinking of new objections or get bored.

However, as we said at the beginning of this chapter, there is no golden rule which says that the salesman must always go through his whole sales offer before he can attempt to close. Whenever he perceives buying signals he should know there is an opportunity to close. It does not matter if the meeting has been in progress five minutes or five hours.

The trial close enables the salesman to check in a positive way if he is picking up the buyer's signals. This close can be used throughout the sales offer to:
— test the buyer's reactions;
— uncover objections;
— determine buyer interest;
— speed the sale;
— help retain the initiative.

This is how it works. During the sales interview the buyer will often ask questions such as:

> 'Can I delay my pension payment until the end of the year?'
> 'Will I get a discount if I pay promptly?'
> 'Can my investment be arranged to give me income for the next couple of years and then be switched for capital appreciation?'

The average salesman will generally respond with a rather lame 'Yes', thus missing a superb opportunity to gain a commitment from the buyer. The skilled salesman responds differently.

Buyer: 'Can I delay my pension payments until the end of the year?'

Salesman: 'Yes. Being self-employed, you can delay payment until you have completed your end-of-year accounts. Is this what you would like to do?'

and

Buyer: 'Will I get a discount if I pay promptly?'

Salesman: 'Yes. If you pay within 30 days we will give a 5% discount. Is that how you would like to pay?'

Notice how the skilled salesman asks another question in reply, thereby learning much more about the buyer and his readiness to purchase.

Forcing questions

The salesman can use forcing questions with similar effect. For example, on perceiving a buying signal he could respond as follows:

'You would prefer to delay your pension payments until later, wouldn't you?'

'You will want to take advantage of our bonus discount for prompt payment, won't you?'

Using this technique the salesman makes an assumption based on the buyer's signals and puts a question to which 'yes' would seem to be the only sensible answer.

Questions like these, designed to obtain commitments from the buyer, start and end with particular words:

'You do . . . don't you?'
'You will . . . won't you?'
'It is . . . isn't it?'

Direct questions

It is also possible to seek agreement on minor points by asking direct questions:

'Do you want a life cover policy without profits?'

'Do you want us to advertise your house in this weekend's papers?'

Clearly, questions such as these can receive either a 'yes' or 'no' response. However, the merit of the trial close is that a negative

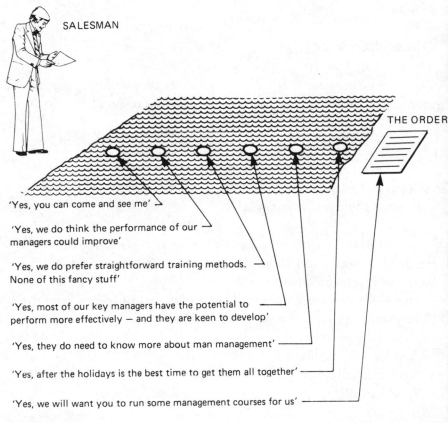

SALESMAN

THE ORDER

'Yes, you can come and see me'

'Yes, we do think the performance of our managers could improve'

'Yes, we do prefer straightforward training methods. None of this fancy stuff'

'Yes, most of our key managers have the potential to perform more effectively — and they are keen to develop'

'Yes, they do need to know more about man management'

'Yes, after the holidays is the best time to get them all together'

'Yes, we will want you to run some management courses for us'

Figure 11

response is not a disaster. The salesman has lost little if a minor point is not acceptable to the buyer. He can continue with his sales offer and try to close again later.

Even a negative response to a trial close can provide the salesman with some useful insights about the buyer's attitudes and values.

By using trial closes the salesman can accumulate a series of small commitments throughout the interview, which taken together win the order. They can be likened to stepping stones across a stream.

Alternative closes

Sometimes it is preferable not to ask questions which force the buyer into making a 'yes/no' answer because, as we have already discussed, a negative response can create a difficult situation for the salesman. Once an opinion is voiced it is not easy for the salesman to persuade the buyer to change his mind.

An alternative close neatly avoids forcing the buyer into giving a 'yes' or 'no' answer by, in effect, asking him to choose between two 'yes' propositions. It works like this:

'Would you prefer to pay monthly or quarterly?'

'Will you want the insurance scheme with or without profits?'

'Do you want us to make arrangements next week, or the week after?'

Note the implied assumption that the buyer will obviously want the service. Once the buyer has stated his preference, then the salesman can close the sale by asking for the order.

The alternative close is particularly useful in helping a hesitant buyer to make up his mind. Similarly, it can be used when the buyer is not giving clear buying signals.

Summary closes

Again this form of close can be useful when faced with a hesitant

buyer because it is a way to:
– convince him that he wants the service;
– convince him your sales offer is better than a competitor's;
– bring a sales offer to a conclusion.

There is a slight variation in the closing technique in each of these cases.

Convincing the buyer that he wants the service When a buyer is unconvinced whether or not to buy, the salesman can offer to help him summarize the pros and cons of making the purchase.

What the salesman then does is to take a sheet of paper and draw a line down the centre from top to bottom. On the left-hand side of the paper he writes the heading 'Advantages' and on the right-hand side, the heading 'Disadvantages'.

With the buyer, the salesman starts to list all the advantages stemming from the service itself and the sales offer. After a few minutes an impressive list of advantages ought to appear and clearly outnumber the disadvantages.

After allowing enough time for this information to make impact on the buyer, the salesman can say something like:

'Well, there seems to be a very strong case for buying our service Mr Buyer. What is your opinion now?'

Convincing the buyer that our sales offer is better than a competitor's The salesman follows a similar procedure to that given above. However, the headings this time become 'Our service/offer' on the left and 'Their service/offer' on the right.

Clearly the salesman is in a strong position to influence the number of advantages that appear in the left-hand column. In fact he should start by building up this list and only when it looks impressive should he and the buyer turn their attention to the competitor's column.

Without the competitor's salesman being there, it is unlikely that so many advantages will be found for the competing offer.

This technique can be very effective to counter a price disadvantage, when the salesman can summarize like this:

'Well Mr Buyer, as you can see, we are not as cheap as XYZ Supply Services, but look at all the extra advantages you get by dealing with our company. What do you think now?'

Note that the choice of words focuses on the 'cheapness' of the competition rather than the 'expensiveness' of the salesman's own service.

Bringing the sales offer to a conclusion The *straight summary* is slightly different again. This time the salesman makes a verbal summary of the main benefits offered by his service. He need not enumerate each one as this can be time-consuming. Instead, by concentrating on just four or five main customer benefits, the salesman can bring the interview to a speedy and business-like conclusion.

Whichever of these closes is used, the salesman ought to conclude the summary by *asking for the order*.

Concession closes

In the very first chapter of this book we saw how the salesman has several different roles to play in the course of his work and at times he becomes less of a salesman and more of a negotiator.

As we said, negotiation involves a process of give and take by both parties. Therefore, during the interview it might be appropriate for the salesman to give a concession in return for an order or, better still, a larger order from the buyer.

However, there are usually limits to the concessions which the salesman may give and often these are laid down as company policy. Examples of typical concessions are:
– price discounts for large orders;
– extended guarantee periods;
– extended credit;
– generous trade-in allowances;

— free delivery;
— free consultancy;
— free user-training;
— free starter packs or samples;
and so on.

Many salesmen fall into the trap of making the concession too early in the interview. While there is an obvious temptation to introduce it in the opening, in an attempt to interest the buyer, it is wrong to do so for the following reasons:

1 The buyer will not have heard the sales offer at that stage and until he has, he might be unclear about how the service will benefit him.
2 The salesman will have had no time to identify buying signals and check that the concession actually has value in the buyer's mind.
3 It is obviously a sales ploy and will put the buyer on the defensive.

However, later in the interview, when the buyer is in possession of the facts and in a position to weigh up the various advantages and disadvantages of the offer, the salesman might be able to introduce a concession which will finally sway the outcome.

A concession close could operate like this:

'Mr Buyer, I am convinced that this insurance policy will safeguard the interests of both you and your family in just the way you want. However, as an added incentive for you to order, I can give you a reduction on the first year's premium if you sign this application form now. You would like to take advantage of this special offer, wouldn't you?'

A positive reply will usually lead directly to an order.

Quotation closes

There will be occasions when the salesman will be invited to submit a quotation for the service he offers. Indeed in some service industries submitting a quotation is a norm for conducting business.

What is often overlooked is the fact that the sales process is not over (no order has yet been taken), therefore the quotation itself has to be a selling document.

Many potential orders have been lost because the salesman saw the request to submit a quotation as the end of the sales process and consequently broke some cardinal rules listed below. Generally the process of submitting quotations can be improved by following these steps:

1   *Gather all the facts* The salesman has the responsibility of collecting all the necessary facts upon which the quotation will be based. This means that he should use a checklist as he gathers the information and make special notes about any ways the service will deviate from standard offers.

If he is ever in doubt about any point, the salesman should get back in contact with the buyer to confirm the customer's exact requirements.

Often the actual quotation is prepared in the sales office using the salesman's report as the main information source. Where this is the case, the salesman should study his written report and ask himself, 'If I received this, would I have sufficient data to prepare a quotation?'

2   *Submit a proposal with the quotation* A quotation is rarely designed as a selling tool, indeed its basic purpose is to establish the specification for the fulfilment of the order, i.e. price, availability, payment, terms, quality, standards and conditions. As a result, most businessmen treat the quotation as a legal document – and very forbidding it can be at times, written in old-fashioned stilted language and reeling off numerous conditions with which the customer must comply.

Not surprisingly then, quotations often seem to emerge as documents which almost invite the customer *not to order*.

Here is a list of typical expressions that keep cropping up in quotations. They speak for themselves:

'Dear Sirs'
'We thank you for your esteemed enquiry . . .'
'Price will be . . .'
'The service will be made available ten days from receipt of your confirmation to accept this contract'
'Terms of payment nett on invoice'
'Prices hold good for 30 days only from date of this quotation'
'. . . subject to the terms and conditions stated overleaf'
'. . . payment to be completed before services provided'
'. . . the company reserves the right to . . .'
'We trust that the above quotation is to your satisfaction'

It is therefore good practice to submit a *selling proposal* with the quotation. This can be much less formal and can be sent as a covering letter addressed to the buyer in person. (But always use Dear Mr . . . The first name will be too familiar in this instance.)

A good proposal will:
— summarize the supplier's understanding of the customer's requirements;
— describe what is being offered to meet that requirement, in a way which keeps technical language or jargon to a minimum;
— summarize the benefits to the customer. (Note: features alone are not sufficient, any feature mentioned should have an attendant benefit);
— explain the financial justification and the financial benefits to the customer, for example, increased efficiency, reduced cost and so on;
— list any concessions, guarantees or after-sales service.

3   *Follow-up* The salesman should always follow up the quotation with a visit to:
— answer any queries;
— ask for the order.

The follow-up ought to be positive, in the way we recommended when we talked about 'openings' in Chapter 3. It should never be of the 'any news yet' variety. Not only is this a weak opening, but it also betrays the salesman's lack of confidence.

When all else fails . . .

Sometimes, in spite of all his efforts, the salesman just cannot close the sale. He has been calling on the buyer for months, given a comprehensive sales offer and still the buyer is undecided. What should the salesman do?

There is a great temptation for the salesman to cut his losses and abandon all thoughts of ever making a sale to that particular buyer. Yet, even though such doubts start creeping in, there is still one closing technique the salesman can try. It is perhaps the most powerful weapon in his armoury – the *straight question*.

'What do I need to do to get you to buy from us?'

Such a question puts the onus on the buyer to disclose his reasons for not committing himself and more often than not, paves the way to the final close.

Common pitfalls

The salesman is often so concerned about his own presentation and feelings that he has little energy to spare to consider how the buyer is feeling during the sales interview. Through this over-concern about himself and not the buyer, the salesman becomes his own worst enemy, creating needless barriers between himself and the buyer. Here are some very common pitfalls that need to be avoided.

Talking too much

This might be an outward sign of the anxiety the salesman feels at his meeting with buyers. It might just be a bad habit. But whatever the reason, the salesman must learn to control himself if he is talking too much.

Not only will the buyer become disinterested if faced with a lengthy monologue, but also the salesman is missing the opportunity to hear the buyer's views and pick up valuable buying signals.

Not asking questions

The failure to ask questions is a shortcoming among average salesmen. Yet, paradoxically, only by asking questions will the salesman begin to develop buyer commitment and be able to progress towards a close.

Not giving proof

If the salesman is going to sell benefits in the way we have advocated, then he must have supporting materials to back up any claims he might make. Such evidence can be in the form of figures, data charts, surveys, independent reports, newspaper articles, samples and so on.

Not only should these substantiate the salesman's claim, but they should also serve to stimulate and maintain the buyer's interest. It will be impossible for any salesman to close the sale if the buyer is still doubtful or disinterested.

Not listening

Many salesmen only half hear what the buyer says because they are too busy working out what they are going to say next. As a result they miss some very important buying signals. Similarly the buyer will resent his remarks not being picked up. To him, not listening comes over as insensitivity and the resentment can soon cool to disinterest.

Failing to attempt trial closes

Trial closes force the salesman to ask the buyer questions, which means in effect that the salesman reduces the amount of his own talking. Only by working at trial closes will the salesman be able to test the buyer's reactions and level of interest, uncover objections and retain the initiative.

Not asking for the order

The most unpardonable sin of all.

The close

The moment of the close can be a very testing time for a salesman. It can be likened to the angler trying to land a prize catch – one false move and the chance can be lost, perhaps for ever.

How the salesman behaves at this critical phase of the sale can therefore have a significant bearing on the outcome. Here are some useful tips.

1 The salesman should remain silent once he has *asked for the order*. The silence that follows is a measure of the buyer's thinking time. If the silence becomes unbearable (often what seems an interminable age is in reality generally only a few seconds) then the salesman can repeat his request for the order. He should not change the subject. The onus is now on the buyer to make the next move.
2 The salesman should not look surprised or overjoyed when the customer says 'yes'. The competent salesman who has prepared well will have expected no other result and he should react accordingly. A brief thank-you and a confidence building remark, to the effect that the buyer will be pleased with his purchase, will normally suffice.
3 The salesman should leave as quickly as he decently can after

obtaining the order. Further social chat or a cup of coffee before departing is unnecessary and, remember, further discussion can give the buyer an opportunity to think of another objection or perhaps to change his mind.

What happens if there is no sale?

It would be unrealistic to expect every sales interview to be successful. Even with all the preparation that we have suggested, from time to time there will be no sale. The successful salesman tries to learn from this failure rather than put it down to bad luck. He analyses what happened and tries to identify where he might have made a mistake. By doing this he gets new insights about how he can improve his performance.

In conducting this personal post-mortem, he will ask himself questions such as:
— did I have a clear objective for the visit?
— was he really a prospect?
— does he deal with a competitor and if so, who and why?
— does the competition have benefits in their service which ours could not provide?
— did I show and prove all the benefits?
— did I quote for what the buyer asked, or for what I found out he needed?
— did I notice his buying signals?
— what feedback did I receive?
— did I listen to what the buyer said?
— did we send a quotation with a written proposal?
— did I genuinely answer his objections?
— did I provide the necessary proof?
— did I ask for an order?
— did I ask why he did not buy from me?

Success

The successful close is the culmination of a great deal of preparation, planning and hard work. It is the moment that makes it all worthwhile. But the close is not the end of the matter, it is just a step in a continuous process. Once a customer has been gained, then he or she can be lost if for any reason they are dissatisfied with the service offered them. Therefore the salesman must always remember that his objective is not only to close the sale, but to open up a lasting relationship with the customer. In the final analysis, this is what makes a successful salesman.

Application questions

1   Give examples of buying signals. Which ones are most promising in your particular business? How do you follow them up?

2   How many different types of trial close do you typically use?
    a) *If* you use a range of different trial closes, do any particular ones seem to be more successful than others?
    b) *If* you tend only to use one or two types of trial close, can you now begin to see where others might be used to advantage? What are they and how will you use them?

3   Give an example of the following trial closes and explain how you follow them up:
    – the summary close;
    – the concession close;
    – the alternative close;
    – the quotation close.

4   How easy do you find it to ask for the order? If you do not find it to be very easy, what factors inhibit you? How might you work to reduce these factors and thereby improve your effectiveness? Who can you talk to who will give you encouragement and support?

5   What do you find to be the best questions to ask yourself when
    you reflect on situations where you failed to make a sale?

Exercises

Exercise 6.1:   *Opportunities to close*

As you have read in Chapter 6 the successful salesman does not try
to go right through his prepared presentation come what may.
Instead, he is constantly on the look out for short cuts that lead to a
close, or as we have called them, buying signals. It is not always easy
to recognize a buying signal when it crops up and yet to be
successful, we have to learn not only to spot the signal immediately,
but also to respond in a natural sounding way quite spontaneously.

This exercise will enable you to practise the skills of identifying
opportunities to close and working out the best way to respond to
them.

Read 'The Garden Wall' case study below and answer these
questions:

1   Did Derek James, the salesman, miss any buying signals and
    hence opportunities to close the sale?
2   If he did, at which stage or stages of the interview did
    opportunities occur?
3   If you had been in Derek James' shoes, how would you have
    responded to the buying signals you identified in 2 above?

Write your answers down on a separate sheet of notepaper and
when you are satisfied with what you have written, turn to page 256
and check how your answers compare with ours.

The Garden Wall

Derek James was a jobbing builder who undertook a variety of work, from building home extensions to relatively minor house repairs and alterations. Most of his jobs were generated by an advertisement he placed regularly in the local newspaper, the rest by word of mouth.

It was through the former medium that Colin Barrett had got to know of James. Barrett was looking for someone to build a decorative wall in the garden of his home. In pursuit of this he had contacted three local builders with a view to comparing their estimates for the job.

James was the first of the three to be seen. Barrett's initial impressions in talking to James over the phone were completely favourable and unbeknown to James he was already a strong candidate for obtaining the order. It all now depended on how he handled the sales interview. What follows is a transcript of that meeting.

James: 'Hello, Mr Barrett? I'm Derek James. You wanted to talk to me about some building work.'

Barrett: 'Ah yes. Thank you for coming so promptly. Now what I'm looking for is a small decorative retaining wall round that section of raised garden over there. (He points to the area.) Can you give me an estimate for how much it will cost?'

James: 'Certainly . . . and I don't charge for giving an estimate. But I need to know a little bit more about the job first. For example, do you have a special type of brick or colour in mind?'

Barrett: 'Actually we're not too sure. My wife would prefer to have bricks that match the rest of the house. I would really prefer something a little more rustic.'

James: 'Well, let me try to help you. If you use normal housebricks like the others, they are only made to "weather" on the face. If they are used as a retaining wall, there is a problem that they soak up water and when the frosts come they start to flake and crack. Ornamental bricks on the other hand don't absorb water – but they are much more expensive.'

Barrett: 'Oh dear! I didn't really want to spend too much. After all we don't live out in the garden do we?'

James: 'Yes, I understand Mr Barrett. But the ornamental bricks will last for ages and they will provide a most attractive feature in your garden.'

Barrett: 'Mmm. Are these bricks easy to get hold of? Now that we've made up our mind to do something, we would like to get things moving quickly.'

James: 'I'd imagine they would be in stock, unless you wanted something quite unusual. Generally the capping pieces need to be ordered though. That might cause a delay.'

            pause

Barrett: 'Well, getting back to the bricks idea. Can anything be done to stop them absorbing water?'

James: 'Yes. I was going to say that if a plastic sheet is used between the bricks and the retained soil it acts rather like the damp proof course of a house and keeps the bricks dry.'

Barrett: 'Is that expensive to do?'

James: 'Not really, but with bricks you will need some form of capping to stop the rain soaking in at the top.'

Barrett: 'Is this the stuff that has to be ordered specially?'

James: 'Oh no! This is readily available. No problems with that.'

pause

'Just a minute though, I've just remembered that one of the builders merchants is doing a special promotion on ornamental walling. I could probably pick up the ornamental bricks at a reduced price.'

Barrett: 'Oh dear! I was just beginning to get away from the idea of ornamental walling because of the cost. Now I'm back where I started. (He sighs.) I'm really quite confused.'

James: 'Well, Mr Barrett. It's not for me to tell you what you should have. I think it has to be a personal choice. After all you're the ones who will have to look out at the wall every day.'

Barrett: 'I suppose you're right. I'll have to discuss it with my wife when she gets back from her sister's. It's a pity really, I was hoping to get things moving.'

James: 'Never mind. It can't be helped. You do need to be certain in your own minds about something like this. Let me know when you have decided what you want and I'll come round and give you a quote.'

They shook hands. James retreated down the garden path leaving Barrett standing alone staring glumly at the patch of raised garden, trying in his mind's eye to visualize it surrounded with a decorative wall.

Exercise 6.2: *The quotation*

As we have seen, there are various ways of closing the sale. One technique which is widely used in selling a professional service is to submit a quotation. However, while a well-written quotation can go a long way towards closing the sale, a poorly prepared one can end all possibilities of making progress.

Many salesmen fight shy of submitting a written proposal because intuitively they sense that when set down in black and white, their sales proposition does not stand up to close scrutiny. They suddenly realize how little they know about the prospective client and his situation.

This exercise is designed to give you practice at submitting a written quotation – one which tries to close the sale.

Instructions

1   Read the background information to 'the quotation' which follows.
2   Imagine that you are Dennis Hunt (the salesman). Write a letter to Frederick Taylor, the prospective client, with the objective of getting him to agree to buy your service.
3   When you are satisfied with the letter you have written, check it against the suggestions provided on page 258.

The quotation

Dennis Hunt has just come away from a relatively friendly but businesslike meeting with Frederick Taylor, a self-employed builder and decorator who in turn has a network of people he employs from time to time. He had been trying to convince Taylor that he (Hunt) should prepare his end of year accounts, take care of all his tax matters and also provide financial management advice throughout the year.

Hunt had recently left a large firm of chartered accountants and was busy building up his own clientele. He did in fact have considerable expertise in dealing with the financial affairs of small companies.

For his part Taylor was receptive to the idea of 'off-loading' all his paperwork – a part of the job he loathed. Nevertheless, he was a cautious man and watched his spending very carefully. When he heard Hunt mention that this financial service would occupy something like five days of his time per year, his instinct told him that this could be an expensive service to buy into.

As a delaying tactic he had asked Dennis Hunt to put it all in writing so that he could study the offer at leisure.

Task brief

You are Dennis Hunt. You believe that you could probably charge Taylor about £650 + V.A.T. + expenses for the financial services you can provide. Write your letter to Taylor.

Exercise 6.3:   Does persistence pay?

From all the foregoing work it is easy to see that if a salesman applies himself to a sensible approach to planning and then uses some of the sales techniques we have described he ought to improve his performance. But are techniques about planning and tips about handling a sales interview enough? Perhaps there is something more.

Read the story which follows, a true story incidentally, and see if you can relate it to a sales situation. Afterwards, try answering the questions posed at the end of the story.

Does persistence pay?

On a recent TV chat show, Beryl Reid the actress told the story about how she got her 'big break' into show business. This is what happened.

After a period of modest success with her early career in the provinces, she came to London determined to get a part in a forthcoming pantomime. She had no contacts and little money.

She took 'digs' in a very cheap rooming house in Brixton and to save money walked to Tom Arnold's office in Shaftesbury Avenue. (He was a most important impresario of the time.) On arriving, Miss Reid asked to see Mr Arnold but was informed by his secretary that unless she had an appointment it would be impossible. 'Mr Arnold is such a busy man.' The young actress refused to take no for an answer, 'I'll wait here until he will see me then.' With that she sat down on a chair in the waiting room. She was ignored for the rest of the day and had to leave when the office closed.

At 9.00 a.m. the next morning she was back in the waiting room. Another uneventful day passed and she found herself trudging back to Brixton. In fact she spent three weeks following this routine, by which time she was running low both in hope and money. The only bright spot was that the secretary now offered her cups of tea during the day.

Eventually Tom Arnold could stand seeing her there no longer, an ever waiting figure outside his office. He granted Beryl Reid an interview at which her cheek, tenacity and talent impressed him so much that he gave her a part in one of his productions. This proved to be the turning point in her career.

Are there any lessons that salesmen can learn from this story?

Questions

1 What are the positive points from this story?
2 What are the negative points from this story?
3 Write your answers on a separate piece of notepaper and when you have finished, compare them with the suggestions given on page 261.

Exercise 6.4:   The post mortem

We can't make a sale every time, but when we fail we should always try to discover what went wrong.

Without referring back to the main text, make a list of all the points on which a salesman ought to assess himself when conducting a personal 'post mortem'. Make it a personal list by using 'I', e.g., was *I* enthusiastic?

When your list is complete, check it with the one on page 263. Finally study your list and highlight the points to which you will need to pay particular attention at your next sales interview.

Model Answers

Chapter 1

Exercise 1.1: True or false quiz

1 *False* – A product can be made to an agreed physical specification, a service cannot. Thus the element of trust figures high in the purchase of a service.

2 *False* – Modified re-buys provide a superb opportunity to re-examine the buy phases and re-activate component parts of the decision making unit.

3 *False* – There is invariably a product element for any service e.g. a report from a house survey, a smarter house from a decorator, etc.

4 *False* – In the long run the salesman must strive to develop a bank of new prospects because existing clients will eventually 'dry up'. (In the short term it is often a fruitful strategy to look for extra business from existing clients.)

5 *True* – Since it is difficult to specify a service as rigorously as a product, the salesman's knowledge and expertise becomes a key part of the sales offer.

6 *True* – It is difficult for individuals in a company system to own up to buying on 'emotional grounds', thus rationality tends to prevail.

7a *True* – The buyer can be a useful ally.

7b *False* — Other components of the D.M.U. might have more
power.
8 *True* — With greater selling skills a salesman will be more
understanding of the buyer's situation, concentrate
on real benefits to the buyer, be more lucid and
persuasive in making his presentation *and* close the
sale.
9 *False* — There is little supporting evidence that 'entertaining'
determines the placing of a contract.
10 *True* — Good negotiators are prepared to move from one
issue to another in no set pattern.

Note: If you had more than two answers wrong, it would be
advisable for you to re-read Chapter 1 before proceeding.

Exercise 1.2: *What needs do you want your job to satisfy*

Before the scores can be interpreted, it will be necessary to have
some understanding about the theory at the heart of this motivation
questionnaire.

It has been long held that much of man's behaviour can be
explained in terms of needs which he experiences. That presence of
an inner need creates a tension or drive within us which does not
disappear until the need is satisfied.

Thus, if I feel hungry, the need for sustenance will have a direct
bearing on my actions and will keep nagging away at me until I go
out and find food.

Similarly, if I had a deep felt need to impress the neighbours, it
might cause me to go and buy an expensive car and flaunt it in the
drive outside.

So when we talk about somebody being motivated, we generally
mean that he is demonstrating some kind of purposeful behaviour,
which is almost certainly in accord with his inner needs.

Abraham Maslow

Abraham Maslow was an American clinical psychologist who became very interested in studying what motivated his clients. As a result of his studies he concluded that there seemed to be a hierarchy of different types of needs.

Basic needs   The first level of needs he called basic needs. These are all physiological in origin and are concerned with necessities for survival, such as the need for food, water, air, warmth, shelter and so on.

It could be argued that in advanced countries all citizens have a standard of living that takes these things for granted. But perhaps this is only a thin veneer. At times of war, natural disasters or national shortages, say as a result of industrial action, basic needs come to the fore as people develop strategies for survival such as hoarding food or stockpiling coal.

Security needs   Once a person has satisfied his basic needs, he has the physical and psychological energy to put into satisfying other needs. This next level is termed security needs. They are in essence about safeguarding one's interests from the attacks of others in order to obtain enduring satisfaction from them. Creating conditions of personal safety free of uncomfortable ambiguity, could well feature for a person operating at this level.

What this means for a salesman's job we will see later.

Belonging needs   Man is a social animal and once his basic needs are met and he feels reasonably secure in the context of his particular 'world', he begins to recognize the need to meet and interact with others. There is a need to feel that one is part of something.

Ego-status needs   Eventually, it is not enough to be always seen as a face in the crowd or a cog in a machine. A need for individuality starts to exert itself. One wants to be seen as someone special and be recognized for the skills and achievements one brings to the community, be it family, work or neighbourhood.

Self-actualization   Much of the ego-status seeking is done to achieve recognition in the eyes of others *in their terms*. Eventually there comes a time when even that ceases to satisfy, because deep-down one realizes that there is still so much more untapped potential within oneself. One senses that there is a need to be more creative, to take charge of one's life and to become the best 'me' that I could possibly become.

This was the highest level of needs that Maslow identified. Whereas the basic needs were physiological in origin, these higher needs are deeply psychological, but nonetheless real for that.

Diagrammatically we could show these different levels of need as a hillside, with basic needs at its foot.

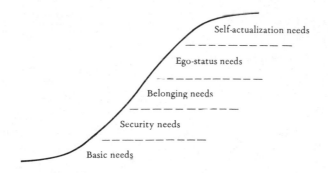

The hillside analogy is quite useful for another reason. Maslow postulated that if a person was blocked or challenged at one level of the hierarchy, he could in fact slide down the slope and find himself at another. For example, a sales manager with high needs for self-actualization believes that the only solution to his problem is to join another company, where the job would have much greater scope for him to use his talents.

He changes jobs then finds that he is somewhat exposed in this new setting and doesn't fully understand what is going on around him. To make life more predictable he begins to introduce some of the systems with which he was familiar at his old job. He also entices one or two of his former colleagues to join him.

Far from self-actualizing, his behaviour is now driven by a resurgence of security needs. Even when these are met, it might still take some time for the belonging and ego-status needs to be satisfied. This explains why very often a manager experiences problems when he changes jobs. Often, as in this example, the transition can take several months before the manager might get round to functioning in a fully autonomous manner.

It is possible to identify different concerns in a sales setting which are analogous to the levels of needs put forward by Maslow.

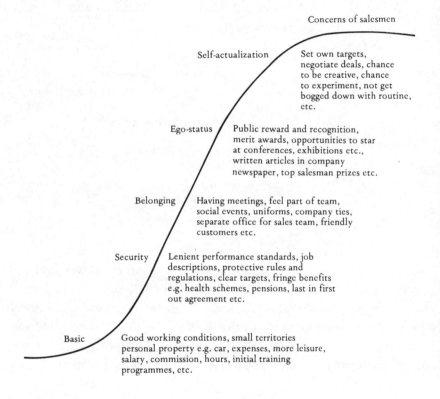

Concerns of salesmen

Self-actualization — Set own targets, negotiate deals, chance to be creative, chance to experiment, not get bogged down with routine, etc.

Ego-status — Public reward and recognition, merit awards, opportunities to star at conferences, exhibitions etc., written articles in company newspaper, top salesman prizes etc.

Belonging — Having meetings, feel part of team, social events, uniforms, company ties, separate office for sales team, friendly customers etc.

Security — Lenient performance standards, job descriptions, protective rules and regulations, clear targets, fringe benefits e.g. health schemes, pensions, last in first out agreement etc.

Basic — Good working conditions, small territories personal property e.g. car, expenses, more leisure, salary, commission, hours, initial training programmes, etc.

Frederick Hertzberg

Frederick Hertzberg, another American, this time a behavioural scientist who has completed many assignments in industry concerned with improving motivation. In essence, Hertzberg modified the ideas put forward by Maslow in the following way.

1 He proposed that when it came to looking at 'real' motivation, it was really only the top levels of Maslow's hierarchy that worked. Only the striving for self-actualization and some aspects of ego-status were likely to produce 'motivated performance' from which the company would benefit.

2 The lower levels were not motivators as such, but satisfiers. If people's needs were not met at the lower levels then they became dissatisfied. However, by removing the dissatisfiers it meant that people were no longer dissatisfied, which in Hertzberg's terms was a long way from being motivated.

3 He likened the hierarchy of needs as going to a hospital. The real purpose was to cure the patient, but while he was in hospital it was essential to ensure that a level of hygiene was observed to ensure the patient didn't contract any new diseases or get worse. Thus the real purpose of a motivation system ought to be to do just that, provide motivation. However, at the same time the company must not allow the potential dissatisfiers, or hygiene factors to get in the way.

4 Diagrammatically the connection between Maslow's ideas and Hertzberg's seem to be this.

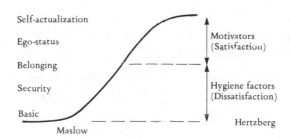

5 Overall what Hertzberg seems to be saying about a company's approach to motivating its staff can perhaps be encapsulated thus:

	Hygiene factors (lower levels)	Motivators (higher levels)
Absent	Staff will be dissatisfied	Staff will not be motivated
Present	Staff will not be dissatisfied	Staff will be motivated

6 The final point to observe in these brief notes is the fact that
   when a company concentrates on the lower levels of need
   motivation, most of the concerns will need money or resources
   to be provided, if they are to be overcome. *Note*, remember to
   provide motivation, just to avoid dissatisfaction. In contrast,
   many of the concerns which could be addressed at the higher
   level, for example, giving praise and recognition for a good job
   well done, involve little expenditure and can in fact lead to
   highly motivated individual performance from which the
   company could expect concrete and worthwhile results.

Interpretation of scoring

By now you will have probably realized that the various boxes A–E
you scored in Part 2 of the questionnaire equate to the five types of
needs put forward by Maslow. A being basic needs; B, security; C,
belonging; D, ego-status and E, self-actualization.

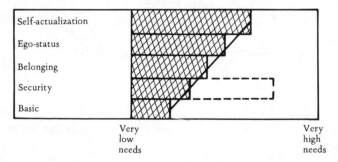

The chart in which you placed your scores shows diagrammatically the degree to which you appear to be 'motivated' by the various levels of need.

There are of course no 'right' answers to the questionnaire. All one can do is to interpret the relative strength of the needs you scored.

There is quite a lot of evidence to suggest that most successful sales people would have a score profile rather like the example shown on the diagram. *Not* necessarily in the same position, with the same order of scores, but certainly showing a gradually increasing score for each level on the Maslow hierarchy.

We will all have our own profile, but what should interest us are any scores that are unduly high and distort the slope of a line that could be drawn through all the score lines on your chart in Part 3 of the questionnaire (such as the dotted line shown in the diagram (page 218), where security needs seem unduly high).

The foregoing theory will have given us some clues about what unduly high scores might mean.

High basic score

This indicates that you have a very high concern for the 'creature comforts' of the work. By themselves these are not motivators, but you will be looking for someone to create the right environment for you.

A high score here might also indicate that your personal circumstances put you under pressure e.g. high mortgage or outgoings.

You will not be in a mood to throw yourself into your work, unless there is the prospect of more money for your efforts.

High security score

This indicates that you probably prefer to 'go by the book' and 'play it safe'. The high score suggests that you would want your working life to be well ordered, predictable and with a safe and secure future.

You must ask yourself whether or not this high needs score would be compatible with a career in selling.

Again like the high basic needs scorer, you will be dependent upon others to motivate you. It is possible that a 'stick' will be a more powerful motivator than a 'carrot' as far as you are concerned.

High belonging score

A high score here shows that you have a high need for people. Not only will you want signs of their appreciation of you, but you will also show warmth to others.

Your needs to belong might, if not met by your company, cause you to identify much more with your friendlier customers – almost to the extent of seeing yourself as 'part' of their organization; rather than your own.

Because of your high belonging needs, you might well have a preference to 'soft pedal' in a sales situation because of the fear that to ask for an order might damage the relationship with the customer.

You clearly need to feel that you are part of a team.

High ego-status score

You appear to be a person who needs to be respected and feel important. However, in reaching for these goals you are likely to pull out many of the 'stops' and therefore be quite successful in your career.

You will certainly work hard, attracted by the prospect of esteem, recognition and wanting to be the best, to stand out in the crowd. You are ambitious.

However, your energy and drive to meet your own needs could lead you to become insensitive to the customer's needs and in this way be self-defeating. You might well, for example, need to cut down on the talking and improve your listening to be really successful.

High self-actualization score

You would seem to have a strong desire to work independently, be free to make decisions and take much responsibility for your needs to grow and develop.

You are a self-motivating, self-determining sort of person who is prepared to face up to challenges and use creative ideas to overcome problems.

However, remember that this exercise is only investigating your needs (not your capabilities), your personal preferences if you like. Although you might strive for personal autonomy, your technical skills or problem-solving capacity might not yet be sufficiently developed. But you can, and probably will, work at overcoming such deficiencies.

What does this exercise show?

Well, to a large extent it demonstrates where a salesman stands in relation to his job and a possible career in industrial sales, *at this moment.*

Because people can learn and develop, because their situations change, because they grow older and wiser, so can their values and beliefs also change. It follows therefore that these scores are not necessarily fixed. Change is possible given the right environment and support.

What we hope that this exercise does is to illustrate the starting point at which somebody enters into this learning programme. Knowing more about oneself is a prerequisite to working out how one can begin a programme of self-improvement.

*Exercise 1.5:	The easy sale*

1	David Brown had very little to feel pleased about, if only he had realized:

— At the first mention of price, he gave away a 30 per cent discount in return for nothing.

— He has committed Acme Engineering to providing an additional service to Victoria Presses' Northern Plant, without due regard to the costs involved.

— He has agreed to penalty clauses on late delivery at both plants.

2	There were two critical phases of the interview:

(a)	The first was when Jeff Gregory took control by being a listening, low reactive buyer. (David Brown couldn't handle the silences, nor did he ask questions.)

(b)	The second was when Gregory suddenly switched the situation to a negotiation. Brown hadn't appreciated a change of role was called for, he thought getting the sale was enough.

3	David Brown should have had a greater understanding of the value of Acme's service to Victoria Presses in order that he could talk in terms of benefits and hence overcome the 'price' objection. Discounts should only be given as a last resort. Overall, Brown was overconcerned with his own feelings (telling his sales manager, celebrating with his wife) and didn't understand how Gregory was moving the discussion.

4	He didn't know why Victoria Presses wanted to use a new tool repair service after being so happy with their previous supplier. This clearly would have had a key bearing on the whole sales/negotiation interview.

Chapter 2

Exercise 2.4: Writing a sales letter

Having analysed Mr G. H. Bennett's letter to Acme Engineering Co. Ltd you should have made some comments about the following points:

1 *The Addressee*
   Is the Managing Director the person who will be most interested in the service? Might the Financial Director have been a more appropriate recipient? Always use the name of the recipient, even if you have to phone the company to check what it is.

2 *Presentation*
   Nothing in the presentation makes it personal to Acme Engineering. It is obviously a printed 'Yours faithfully' circular and as a result doesn't command much attention.

3 *Content*
   The letter has one or two things to commend it, for example,

   (a) It introduces several important items.
   (b) It has some customer appeal because the writer has personalized it by using the first person singular e.g. 'I have taken over', 'I have taken the opportunity', etc.

   However, overall the letter is fairly dull and lacks punch. (Did it capture your interest?) There are too many weak phrases e.g. 'You may find details of the bank's factoring operations of interest', 'gives an indication', 'it would I am sure'. . . . The final phrase does not invite positive action and contains no lever for selling when the letter is followed up. The last paragraph is terribly stilted English and is a typical example of outdated business language.

4   *Length*

Since the letter was designed to arrange an appointment, it did not need to be as long or as complex as it was. One or two good reasons for a meeting would be enough.

Below is an example of the letter as it might have been written. You will note how reference to a newspaper story is quoted as a lever. (While this lever was 'invented', in your letter some form of lever should be included.)

INTERNATIONAL BANK LIMITED

Commercial Street   Our Ref: GHB/jf
Ourtown
West Midlands
OT2 2LG

Mr R. K. Jones
Financial Director
Acme Engineering Co Ltd
Britannia Industrial Estate
Ourtown
West Midlands

Dear Mr Jones

I have recently taken over the management of the Ourtown Branch of the International Bank. It was my intention to make contact with you in the normal course of business, but having just read about Acme Engineering's success in winning its first export contract, it seemed more appropriate to do so now.

Sorting out the financial arrangements and coping with the mass of documentation and administration procedures can be something of a headache for first time exporters like yourselves.

But they don't have to be.

The International Bank has helped many companies like yours to become thriving exporters. When we combine our expert services with our client's natural business enterprise, it always proves to be a winning formula.

We really ought to meet and discuss the ways our services could save you time and effort and reduce the risks at this exciting stage of your company's development.

I will contact you early next week to check when a meeting would be most convenient.

Yours sincerely

Gordon H. Bennett
Manager

Exercise 2.5:   Securing an appointment

Step 1:   Suggested plan for telephoning Neil Henderson

Opening: Hello, is that Mr Henderson? Good morning Mr Henderson, my name is James Green of Spick and Span Office Cleaning Contractors. Can you spare me a minute? The reason I am ringing Mr Henderson is that . . .

The lever: Mr Evans, your Sales Director, attended a conference last week and met one of our directors. (It is essential before planning the call to get back to the Sales Manager to find out how the lead for Henderson had been established. Whatever the answer it would clearly be a ploy for a 'lever'.) He mentioned that the service provided by your current cleaning contractors left something to be desired and that we ought to contact you.

The close: It wouldn't take long for me to demonstrate to your satisfaction whether or not we could offer a better service at a competitive rate. Can we agree on a time we could meet? How about early morning, then you could show me the state in which you find the offices after they have been 'cleaned'. How about Tuesday or Wednesday morning?

Step 2: *Speaking to the secretary*

When speaking to Henderson's secretary, your approach ought to be something like the following:

'Hello, who is that I'm talking to?'

'Oh, Miss Brown, my name is James Green of Spick and Span, I'm sure you can help me. Mr Evans, one of your directors, has suggested that I ought to meet Mr Henderson about a business matter which could save your company a lot of unnecessary expense. Can you put me through to Mr Henderson or can you make an appointment in his diary for us to meet as soon as possible?'

Step 3: *This is how you might have responded to objections raised by Mr Henderson's secretary*

Possible objections	*Possible counters*
1 'Mr Henderson is tied up this week because he is preparing to be away on holiday for three weeks from next Monday and is busy arranging for others to cover for him.'	'It must be important for us to meet or your director wouldn't have mentioned it. How about early morning before the day really gets going, or late in the day or during lunchtime?'
2 'He only sees representatives on Thursday and Friday afternoons and is fully tied up at those times.'	'Yes, I quite understand. Your Mr Henderson is a very busy man . . . but we could be talking about ways to save your company a lot of money. Surely that justifies making a little exception to the rule. How about if we met . . .?'

ception to the rule. How about if we met . . . ?'

3 'Let me take a message.'

'I wish it could be as simple as that, Miss Brown. Unfortunately, we have to discuss some very complex situations . . . ?'

Step 4: This is how you might have countered Mr Henderson's objections

Possible objections	*Possible counters*
1 'Current contractors say they will improve.'	'I should hope so – but that's no reason for not looking around for comparisons. Who knows, there might be considerable savings to be made.'
2 'Oh, it's not that bad.'	'Your director, Mr Evans, seemed to think it was.'
3 'I don't know much about your company.'	'We are fairly new but already we have among our clients (give examples) and they are very pleased with our services.'
4 'I'm really very busy, I don't think I can find time to meet for a few weeks.'	'I do understand. Yet it would only take a few minutes of your time and it could solve a lot of problems. How about if we aimed to meet after most of your colleagues have left work?'

Chapter 3

Exercise 3.2:   Suggested opening statements

Here are some suggestions about the way you might have opened
the various sales interviews. Remember, these openings are provided as guidelines and your responses do not have to be exactly the
same.

*Situation 1:   You are visiting a client company on the heels of an
advertising campaign in the national press*

'Did you see our advertisement in the . . . Mr Buyer?'

If the response is *yes*:   'Can you tell me how you reacted to it?'
If the response is *no*:   'Well, let me tell you what we are aiming to
                            do.'

The advertisement is a good lever to open the interview. Even a
'no' response can keep the salesman in control of the situation.

Situation 2:   It is your first meeting with the client

'Mr Buyer, as we haven't met before, how would it be if I spent a
couple of minutes telling you about our company, the services we
offer and the impressive results we achieve for our clients? We
could then move on to discuss the ways in which we might be able
to bring you similar benefits.'

At a first meeting the buyer is likely to feel insecure because there
are so many unknowns. This opening removes the insecurity in
three ways:

● It provides the offer of necessary background information.
● It offers a structure to the meeting.
● It does not sound as if the salesman is going to waste time.

Situation 3: You have submitted a proposal to the client company

'Well, Mr Buyer, have you had time to study my proposal?

If the response is *yes*: 'Perhaps you can tell me what you think of it?'

If the response is *no*: 'Never mind, let me quickly go through it then.'

Clients do not always read proposals as quickly as we would like them to. To make this assumption when the client has not read it could be perceived as an attack on him.

The initial question asked pleasantly and non-critically gives rise to two alternatives, either of which can move the sales interview forward and under control.

Situation 4: Your organization has developed a new service

'As you know, Mr Buyer, we have established our reputation by providing a single first-class service. We are now adding another equally fine service to our existing one. Let me tell you about it.'

Talking about the new service in this way reinforces the value of the other earlier service and does not imply that it is now superseded.

Situation 5: Your contact at the company has been loath to commit himself to a decision despite several earlier meetings

'Mr Buyer, I'm pleased that you have taken the time to weigh up all the pros and cons of my proposition. Now, perhaps if we can just summarize where we have got to in our discussion, we can then decide how we can progress matters to a favourable solution.'

This is not criticism of the buyer but recognizes the need to recap the situation and perhaps identify any hitherto unvoiced objection.

It also attempts to involve the buyer in the summarizing process and thereby (hopefully) makes it easier to progress to a close.

Situation 6:   There has been a complaint to head office

'I'm very sorry to hear that you had to complain, Mr Buyer. I'm here to straighten things out if I possibly can. Now as I understand it, what happened was . . .'

The response is genuine in its sorrow. The salesman is being as positive as he can in the circumstances. The buyer is not asked to explain all over again why he is complaining, and the salesman demonstrates that people at head office actually listen to complaints and relay them back to the field.

Situation 7:   You are asked to visit a client company at the request of their buyer

'I'm extremely pleased that you have contacted us, Mr Buyer. Can I ask you how you got to hear of our service? And what is it exactly you would like to discuss?'

If the request is out of the blue it can be helpful to know how it originated – it can sometimes strengthen the salesman's position by having such information. However, it is wise to move on quickly to finding the reason behind the request by asking a simple question.

Situation 8:   The buyer is an extremely busy person

'I know you are extremely busy, Mr Buyer, so let's get to the heart of the matter.'

Sometimes 'busyness' is used by buyers as a screen behind which to hide. However, when the time constraints are genuine, there will be no better way of empathizing with the busy buyer than to manage the interview time well.

Situation 9: You were given a referral to the client by another customer

'Well, Mr Buyer, as he might have told you already, your ex-colleague Mr Hones was so impressed by our service that he recommended me to contact you. He felt we might achieve similar savings in your company.'

Having established the reference source, it is advisable to move on to benefits and business matters as quickly as possible, thus avoiding the possible trap of hearing all about their earlier friendship and social lives.

Situation 10: You want to establish a long-term contract with an established client

'I've been checking back and found that over the last five years we have done quite a lot of business together, but in a very spasmodic pattern. Now, what I'm beginning to think, Mr Buyer, is that if we can work out some way of planning ahead when you are likely to need our services, I could possibly save you a lot of money. This is what I have in mind . . .'

There are factual and logical reasons for changing the spasmodic individual contracts into perhaps a longer term contract. The benefits to the customer are clearly going to be in terms of money saving and perhaps a reduction in peak demands for the bought-in service.

If on reflection your replies are nothing like those suggested here, perhaps it would be useful for you to revise the appropriate section of Chapter 3.

Exercise 3.3: Listening

Before you move on to interpret the way you completed Worksheet 4, read through these brief notes about blocks to good listening.

It has been calculated that we spend something like 70 per cent of our waking time communicating in some form or other. This involves a range of skills, for example reading, writing and talking, but by far the most used skill is listening (which takes up approximately 45 per cent of the time spent communicating).

However, although it is an often used skill, there is a lot of evidence to suggest that without conscious training to improve, it can be an inefficient process.

Studies have been made which have compared the differences between groups of good listeners and poor listeners. Some factors consistently appear that seem to be associated with the poor listeners and it is suggested that by working at these, listening can be improved.

What then are these 'blockages' to good listening?

1   Poor listeners seem to make up their minds at a very early stage that the spoken topic is going to be uninteresting and therefore find an inability to concentrate.
2   Poor listeners seem to concentrate on being critical of the flaws in the speaker's style or mannerisms rather than *what* he is saying.
3   Poor listeners seem to get overstimulated by what they hear. They get excited at what the person begins to say and then start developing their own ideas or thinking up 'good questions' and as a result effectively stop listening. The solution is to hear the person before evaluating what he is saying.
4   Poor listeners tend to listen just for facts, whereas the good listeners tend to try to understand the main ideas or concepts. Interestingly enough, by remembering the main ideas people found they could recall a lot more facts.
5   Poor listeners 'fake' attention. This causes problems at two levels:

    (a) The speaker can't respond to signals.
    (b) Listening is an active process and 'faking' is setting up the wrong physical/psychological body signals.

6 Poor listeners tolerate distractions, they put up <u>with</u> not being able to hear what is being said or fail to complain about distracting background noises or behaviour.

7 Poor listeners have tended to avoid difficult listening situations in the past, for example they have rarely listened to debates or 'heavy' presentations on the radio or television.

8 Poor listeners let emotive words 'bug' them. They start getting annoyed or draw conclusions about the speaker's values simply because of the vocabulary he uses. This can have the effect of distorting the message they are trying to hear.

9 Poor listeners fail to recognize that we can cope with heard information at something like three or four times the speed of normal talking. This means that the brain is in effect inactive for 75 per cent of the listening process and unless conscious efforts are made to direct this spare time in a supportive activity, e.g. continual mental recapping of what has been said, what main issues have been raised, etc., it will start wandering off to other topics.

Interpretation of Worksheet 4

Having read the notes above you will probably be able to guess how to interpret your answers on Worksheet 4. But just in case you have not spotted the connection, use the following instructions to help you with your interpretations.

For Questions 1, 3, 6, 7 and 8 only: The crosses you placed on the scales should be near the *right*-hand end if you are a *good listener*. If this is how you scored yourself then probably your learning need will be to keep practising to maintain this level of listening. If you tended to have crosses on the *left*-hand side of these scales, then they are indicators of *poor listening* skills, and you will need to spend more time practising in these areas to become proficient.

For Questions 2, 4, 5, 9 and 10 only: The polarities have been reversed, and so for these questions *good* listening is denoted by crosses on the *left* and *poor* listening by crosses on the *right*. It makes sense to try to remedy any areas of listening that fall short of the highest possible score. Therefore the development exercises below ought to be helpful to you; if you need further practice.

Development exercises

1   Try listening to 'heavy' debates or long speeches if you previously tried to avoid them.
2   Make a tape recording of a debate. On play-back, stop the tape after each contribution and attempt to summarize/paraphrase what has been said without referring to your notes. Check your accuracy by replaying each contribution.
3   Again, without using notes, ask a friend to tell you about his hobbies, or holiday, his 'pet' hobby horse and as he/she is talking, interrupt from time to time with a summary of what has been said so far. Let the friend comment on the accuracy.
4   Watch a video recording of a film or play with the sound turned off. Do this for about five to ten minutes and then write down your interpretation of what took place, based solely on non-verbal 'listening'. Replay with the sound on to check the accuracy of your observations.

Exercise 3.4:   'A day in the life of . . .'

Here is a list of some of the points you should have picked up from the 'case study'.

Personal health	Too many late nights, parties, over-drinking and over-eating can be detrimental to health and alertness.
Breakfast	It is recommended to have a proper breakfast by most doctors and nutritionalists.

Radio	Can be useful to hear about traffic conditions.
Routine	A routine based on work commitments rather than family commitments should be the rule. Appointments early or late in the day were not considered.
Route planning	Adequate time was needed between appointments.
Opening statement	'Any news about that quotation yet?' is pretty feeble.
Loyalty	Comments about head office, thoughts about his manager and constant concern about the situations vacant columns does not suggest much in the way of loyalty.
Lunch	This was clearly overdone and the reasons behind it were hardly for business.
Drink	Beer, followed by wine, followed by brandy is hardly the best preparation for an afternoon's work.
Phoning for appointments	If done from home, try to ensure there is no background noise. Screaming children, an overheard TV or washing machine noise diminish the salesman's credibility.
Reports	These ought to be an accurate reflection of the day. If they are truthful they can provide valuable information for the company.
Call preparation	These needed to be planned with all available aids (e.g. latest catalogue) at one's disposal.
Cold calls	These need special planning to ensure that the companies are in the right target market,

have the potential need, and the ability to purchase. A connection is useful to succeed with a cold call.

Cancellations   It is courteous to phone ahead giving as much notice as possible.

Exercise 3.5:   The George Reeves story

See how your answers compare with our analysis of the George Reeves story.

Question 1:   Was George Reeves genuinely lucky?

Perhaps. All successful salesmen need an element of luck somewhere along the way, but the difference between the successful salesman and the merely average is that they seem to be able to 'make' their own luck.

A comment attributed to Gary Player, the golfer, some years ago illustrates this point. He was being interviewed and the interviewer remarked that Gary had managed to have one or two lucky breaks after being bunkered and landing in the rough.

'Yes', replied Player 'but I've also noticed that since I've put in some hard practice at getting out of those situations, how much my luck has improved.'

By talking about his work and being genuinely proud about what he did and the results he had achieved, George Reeves made things happen. He was selling all the time. What would have happened if he had kept quiet?

Question 2:   What distinguishes George Reeves from the salesman in 'A day in the life of . . .'?

Almost everything! George Reeves' attitude is clearly different to the other salesman and it shows in a number of ways:

1   He has a much more positive approach to life.
2   He is proud of the service he offers and the results he has achieved.
3   He enjoys his work.
4   He is prepared to talk about what he does at any time, not just between 9.00 am and 5.00 pm. Perhaps intuitively he knows that the more people that know about his work, the greater the number of potential customers.

One of the most potent ways of reaching new clients is through 'referrals'. This can be done in two ways:

1   Passively, i.e. using someone else to recommend your service.
2   Actively, i.e. collecting names of new contacts from existing clients and following them up personally.

Question 3: What personal learning points might there be for you from the George Reeves story?

Only you can answer this question. However, we would strongly recommend that you pay particular attention to deciding if there might be further ways you might develop the positive traits of George Reeves.

Also, consider if you could reach more potential clients if you extended your informal contact 'network' and obtained more referrals.

Chapter 4

Exercise 4.1:   Benefit selling

Your answers to Exercise 4.1 ought to look something like the following

Service	Customer(s)	Benefits
1 Membership of a record club	Lovers of a particular style of music	Cost savings Special recordings unobtainable elsewhere Up to date information about the 'scene' First choice on special offers etc.
2 Luncheon Vouchers	Organizations without their own canteen or catering facilities	Cheaper than setting up own catering, shows company's concern for its staff – better relationship A 'perk' for staff, etc.
3 A holiday in the West Country	A specific socioeconomic group	Value for money Uniqueness of sights, landmarks etc. Ease of travel No language or currency problems compared with . . . etc.
4 An evening class	Local individuals with similar educational or vocational interests	Value for money Can enhance career Can improve one's expertise etc.
5 A personal pension scheme	Reasonably affluent Managerial/professional Self-employed	Tax efficient form of saving Means of maintaining standard of living after retirement Freedom from being 'tied' to a company because of its pension scheme, etc.

6 Career counselling service	Those seeking direction by employment/life style	Jobhunting becomes more focused People will be happier (better matched) in new jobs People see clearer sense of purpose in their lives
7 A library	Large/medium organizations in technological/fast changing industries	Cost effective (resources are gathered in one place and not duplicated) staff are better informed Abstracts can save staff time etc.
8 Personal bookkeeping	Small shops and businesses	Removes administration chores The client can get on with his prime task An experienced 'outsider' with a dispassionate eye can see potential pitfalls and thereby safeguard the business
9 A community health programme	(a) local authority (b) the public	Reduces pressure on local health facilities Potential savings Fitness and health equals (a) longer and less pain ridden life (b) better looks and greater sexual attraction (c) more enjoyment from life
10 Office cleaning service	Industrial or commercial businesses	More effective than employing own staff Expertise means the job is done faster and better Absenteeism is automatically covered i.e. guaranteed service Management time is not taken up with non-productive issues about buckets and brooms for example

Exercise 4.2:   *Features into benefits*

Here are the 'features' which appear on the cards you made. Against each 'feature' some examples of an advantage and a benefit are given.

There are probably enough examples listed here for you to calculate what the advantages and benefits might be for any 'special' features cards that you devised using the blank cards.

Feature	Advantage	Benefit
Technical back-up	• Your technical needs can be accommodated by our specialists • Your technical problems can be readily solved by us	• Which means that your own specialists are left free to get on with their routine work • Which means that your own technical staff do not have to waste valuable time trying to keep up to date with complex technological developments
Multinational company	• You get the same high level of service worldwide • You always have a local contact	• Which means that no part of your business empire fails to benefit from our service • Which means that there is always someone available to help solve your problems, *quickly*
Long-established company	• You can rely on us not to 'disappear' overnight • We have years of experience to put at your disposal	• Which guarantees continuity of services for you • Which means that we don't waste time 'reinventing the wheel', we get results fast

No intermediaries	• Communication chains are shortened	• Which means that you get a quick response directly from us whenever you need it
	• No intermediary commission has to be paid	• Which means that you benefit from the reduced costs, because we pass the savings on to our clients
Range of services	• You can deal with us for all your needs	• Which ensures better communication between us, less paperwork for you and the prospect of an increased discount which we make available to high value customers
	• You can have more than just the basic service	• Which means that you can obtain the added benefits which come from investing in a selected package of our services
Reputation	• You can rely on us	• Because a reputation like ours is only earned by providing the right service at the right price, consistently for our many customers
	• You can join the ranks of our satisfied customers	• Which means that you will also experience the cost savings that accrue from our service that they have

Technologically advanced	• It outstrips all competing services	• Which means that you get all the benefits from its superior speed and efficiency
	• Our services will not become obsolete overnight	• Which means that you can invest, secure in the knowledge that you are not buying a 'white elephant'
Based on market research	• We provide what customers need	• And so you can be sure that you are buying a service that has been very carefully designed to be effective
	• We listen to our customers	• Which means that when you do business with us, *you* get the service that *you really* want
Training provided	• Your staff become the experts	• Which means that your company becomes self-reliant and independent
	• You maximize the full potential of the service	• Thereby achieving the maximum efficiency and savings
Market leader	• You can have confidence in us	• Because we have helped so many companies, in similar situations to your own, to *their* satisfaction
	• We must be very competitive	• Because market leadership only comes from being successful in helping clients like you to overcome their problems and providing value for money

Not complicated	• Your staff will find the service easy to use	• Which means that it will not be necessary to invest in expensive training programmes
	• It is simple to keep running	• And therefore any discontinuities are easily rectified
Our experience	• Stretches back over a number of years	• Which means that you can benefit from our acquired wisdom, because we have learnt from the mistakes we made in the past
	• We know just what is required	• Which means that you get the most practical service and there are no hidden pitfalls
Availability	• We can provide the service virtually straight away	• Which means there is no costly waiting caused by the delay
	• We always provide the service to commence on the promised date	• Which means that you can plan ahead in confidence and integrate the service into your work routines with the minimum of disruption and the maximum of benefit
Flexible financial terms	• You can choose the repayment method which suits you best	• Which means that you can plan your cash flow in advance and not overburden your financial resources
	• Payments can be spread over a period of time	• Which means that you will already be receiving benefits from the service as you are still paying

		for it, thereby making the proposition partially self-financing
Family business	• You are assured of personal service • You don't become just another customer	• And that means the best possible service • Which means we take the time and trouble to provide the exact service you require
Guarantees	• You are safeguarded	• Which means that in effect you get the savings we discussed or the service doesn't cost you a penny
	• Our service never lets anyone down	• So you can plan ahead with certainty
Fee/price	• You get more for less	• Which means that your budget allocation 'stretches further' and gives you more flexibility
	• We are very competitive	• And that means that you will be unlikely to find another supplier who will give you better *value* for money
Originality	• What you buy is unique	• Which means that your company's reputation for being in the vanguard of new developments is enhanced
	• Yesterday's answers are unlikely to be appropriate for today's problems	• Which is why we provide creative and intelligent solutions to help you solve today's complex business problems.

Chapter 5

Exercise 5.3:   Dealing with objections

Your answers to the objections that appeared on the cards you
made should be something like the following. You will have to
judge the quality of your responses to the cards that you devised by
using the examples given here as a model.

1   *'It's too expensive'*
    Well, Mr Buyer, I agree it isn't cheap but let us just reconsider
    the total package that you will be buying. Everything is
    included, whereas our competitors charge extra for the
    additional services. When looked at from this angle it is really
    very good value, don't you agree?

2   *'I'm not prepared to wait that long'*
    I quite see your point Mr Buyer, but we did just agree that our
    service matched all your requirements exactly and at the right
    price. Wouldn't it be a shame to lose all these advantages just
    for the matter of a week or two?

3   *'It isn't quite what I'm looking for'*
    I'm pleased that you are so honest with me Mr Buyer. Now
    how exactly doesn't our service meet your needs?

4   *'We've had bad experiences with your company'*
    I'm sorry to hear that Mr Buyer, but let me assure you that we
    have re-organized our internal systems and the troubles you
    mentioned should never happen again.

5   *'There must be a catch somewhere'*
    I'm glad you should think so Mr Buyer, but there really isn't a
    catch. It's just that we are so much more efficient than our
    competitors. You wouldn't want me to increase the price
    especially for you, would you?

6   '*Your literature is difficult to understand*'
    I'm sorry that you found it difficult to understand. What
    exactly is the information you require?

7   '*Your guarantee is less than your competitor's*'
    Yes, you are right but you can see how our service offers so
    much more than competing ones, can't you Mr Buyer?

8   '*I haven't heard of your company before*'
    Well, most companies start in a small way, but let me assure
    you that we are one of the fastest growing in the industry.
    Already we have clients such as (name them) and they are not
    likely to take risks on the services they buy are they Mr Buyer?

9   '*You are too small to help us*'
    It is true that we are small, Mr Buyer, but we have a successful
    record of helping companies like yours.

10 '*It will be too complicated for our staff*'
    Do you know, that was just what one of our major clients said
    to me the other day. But after his staff had been trained I went
    back to see how they were coping, and they made it look easy.
    Looking around, I can't imagine that his staff are even as
    bright as yours. After all, Mr Buyer, you don't just employ
    anyone here, do you?

11 '*You keep sending different people to see me*'
    I'm sorry you found that disconcerting Mr Buyer, but we went
    through a spell of re-organization which is now completed. I
    will now be your sole contact, will that be all right?

12 '*We are not like your other customers*'
    You are quite right. We find that no two clients of ours are the
    same but we have found that many of the problems they face
    are rather similar. For example, they find competition tough
    and want to do all they can to save on costs. Could you go
    along with that situation Mr Buyer? Well, this is where we
    could help you.

13 *'We are happy with our existing supplier'*
Who are they? Oh yes, they have a good reputation. What I'm suggesting Mr Buyer is not for you to ditch them, but to give us a trial run so that you can compare the relative savings from each service. That makes sense doesn't it?

14 *'We only buy British'*
Well I'll make no bones about it, we are foreign owned. But all the management and staff are British. Even so, I would have thought that you would have wanted to buy what is the best value for your company Mr Buyer.

15 *'We have our own experts'*
I wouldn't have expected less from a company like yours Mr Buyer. But what we find is that company personnel tend to get overcommitted with their routine work and for the introduction of this important new service, our specialist staff would be able to bear the brunt of the work, leaving your staff to keep the wheels turning. That makes sense, doesn't it?

Exercise 5.4:   *The missed sale*

Here are guidelines for your possible responses to the story. There are likely to be three main criticisms of Hopcraft

1 He jumped to conclusions.
2 He pre-judged the situation and thereafter made the 'facts' fit in with his own thinking.
3 He perhaps had the wrong strategy in insisting that Mrs Broderick was present at the interview.

The key issue that caused the sale to be lost hinged on the issue that Broderick ('a proud man') was unsure about the extent to which he could commit himself to an expensive life cover policy. He could not own up to this in front of his wife, because he had tended to make out that his business was flourishing in order not to worry her.

He cared very much for his family and wanted to protect them, but on the other hand he was naturally cautious and would not want to overcommit too much of his uncertain income.

Exercise 5.5:   *Analysis of negotiating style*

The exercise you have just completed is based on a management theory known as the Blake Mouton Grid. It will be important for you to understand this theory if you are going to interpret your results accurately. Here are some notes to help you.

The Managerial Grid, as it was originally called, was first put forward as a model for management behaviour in a book of the same title written by R. R. Blake and J. S. Mouton, published in 1964 by Gulf Publishing Company, Houston, Texas. Since then this model has been found to be capable of adaptation to selling and negotiating situations.

The grid operates on the hypothesis that in any sales negotiating there are two distinctly different major concerns affecting the transaction:

1   The salesman's concern for meeting his personal goals.
2   The salesman's concern for the relationship with the customer.

Robert Blake and Jane Mouton devised a grid with these two concerns as the axes. Furthermore they devised a nine point 'scoring' mechanism that operated thus:

If the salesman's concern for his personal goals or the relationship is high, it merits a 9 score.
If these concerns are minimal, they merit a 1 score.

The grid therefore looks like this:

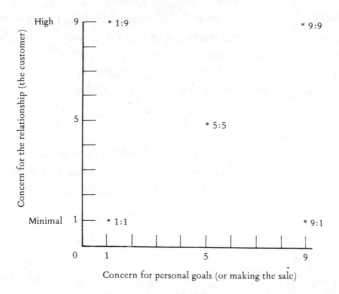

Concern for personal goals (or making the sale)

To understand more about the grid it is important to consider the different characteristics of the key positions shown by the asterisks.

In practice any position on the grid would be possible, but if the student understands the differences between those marked on the diagram, he/she will know how to interpret all other possibilities.

Grid position and negotiating style

9:1 style – high concern for personal goals (sale): low concern for relationship

A salesman with these drives will seek to meet his goals at all costs. For him losing the sale is regarded as a weakness and a blow for his self-image. To succeed gives a tremendous sense of exhilaration and achievement.

There is no doubt in his mind that he is right and will be adept at selecting those facts supporting his position while ignoring all others. He is likely to be high on telling and low on listening.

He will plan to avoid any deviations from his presentation, leave little room for objections to be voiced and be prepared to bend the truth a little, because 'it's the result that counts'.

He will use any power he has to its maximum advantage and not be concerned if the other person has to back down. Under stress he can become very defensive.

As a team leader he will do all the planning, set the rules and tell everyone what they have to do.

- *Strengths:* Being very clear about his personal goals and wanting to achieve results.
- *Weaknesses:* Ultimately, the strengths, which might get some short-term results, become self-defeating. The customers sense the lack of empathy from the salesman and refuse to be pressurized.

1:9 style – minimal concern for personal gains: high concern for relationship

With these drives the salesman will behave very differently from the one above. He will undervalue the achievement of his own goals by being overconcerned about the relationship with the customer. He will abandon his plans if the customer wants to head off in another direction. His main aim is to be accepted by others and not to 'rock the boat'. Thus he will readily accept conditions set by the customer without negotiating trade-offs. Conflict is something the 1:9 seeks to avoid.

He will not use any power he might have in the negotiation. As a team leader, he will bow to the expertise of others and be happy to let them get on with things, providing minimal monitoring of sales progress.

- *Strengths:* He is sensitive to the needs of the relationship and/ or customer. He can provide 'space' and opportunities for self-starting subordinates to develop.
- *Weaknesses:* His minimal concern for results or even his personal goals makes him something of a mystery figure. He readily concedes on any issue so that eventually people stop trusting him because 'they don't know where he stands on anything'. He never stands up for the service or the company if challenged.

1:1 style – low concern for personal goals: low concern for relationship

This style is often the end result of a reasoning process which identifies the need to achieve personal goals and establish relationships, but sees these two requirements as being incompatible. Thus the 1:1 salesman, unlike his 9:1 or 1:9 counterpart, cannot make a choice to favour one concern or the other and psychologically 'drops out'.

Thus his motivation is low, he will only initiate meetings when pushed to do so and will also be reluctant to take risks. This last characteristic is particularly significant, for the 1:1 salesman adopts a low profile in any of his transactions and shows a distinct preference to 'go by the book'.

It must be noted that the 1:1 salesman is not necessarily lazy (his reluctance to take risks ensures that he doesn't leave himself open to this charge) but he will be dependent on being given clear targets and working procedures.

- *Strengths:* There are no obvious strengths emanating from a 1:1 style
- *Weaknesses:* This style encourages a whole range of counter-productive skills which are clearly self-evident from the above test.

5:5 style – medium concern for personal goals (sale): medium concern for relationship

Salesmen operating with this style have more options open to them than any of the foregoing styles. They still have not resolved the apparent conflict between the need for personal goals and the need for relationships but, being less 'hell-bent' in the pursuit of either one of these, they have the flexibility that comes from operating in the middle ground.

Their style could perhaps best be summed up as being prepared to give a little in order to get a little. The 5 score on concern for sale stops them being really high achievers, while the 5 on the relationship scale prevents them really cementing relationships with their customers.

However, this balanced style is difficult to sustain. When under pressure the salesman might easily fall back into 9:1, 1:9 or even 1:1 styles. For this reason, his unpredictability – one minute he is smilingly working at relationship building and then suddenly switches to unsympathetic hard selling tactics – he is something of an enigma to his customers.

- *Strengths:* The salesman will be moderately good at a number of negotiating skills and above all retain an element of flexibility.
- *Weaknesses:* The flexibility demonstrated by the 5:5 sales-man leaves the buyer unsure about how much to trust the salesman.

9:9 style – high concern for personal goals (sale): high concern for relationship
This style is unlike any of the foregoing for one extremely important reason. The salesman who subscribes to the 9:9 style sees no inherent conflict in accommodating both the concern for sale and the concern for relationship. To him it ought to be possible to integrate both of these concerns (at a high level) in all his dealings with customers.

Thus he will plan to achieve the sale but at the same time be genuinely concerned with the customer's viewpoint. He will be truthful in his dealings and see it as legitimate to use power in his transactions. *But* he is always striving for a win-win situation where both parties feel they have got the best possible deal from the negotiation.

He will be aware of stress in himself and others during negotiations and will be prepared to own up to, or show, his feelings. Similarly he would prefer that any conflict is made open and dealt with, rather than remaining as a hidden agenda, implicitly getting in the way of problem solving.

As a team leader the 9:9 salesman will utilize all the resources available to him, being open to well argued proposals from any subordinate. His final choice will be concerned about 'what will be best for our company' and he will be mature enough not to 'stick' on particular issues for reasons of ego-satisfaction.

- *Strengths:* The capacity to harness the high concern for sale with an equally high concern for relationship with the customer. This combination promotes a high level of authentic behaviour which readily communicates to customers.
- *Weaknesses:* The 9:9 salesman can be a hard taskmaster if leading a team because he will set very demanding standards by his personal behaviour. There is a possibility for this salesman to set himself 'impossible' targets and become overobsessed with his failure to meet them.

Relevance of negotiating skills

In practice we all adopt 'a bit' of all of the foregoing negotiating styles but for one reason or another have probably developed a preference for some styles at the expense of others. This might be a good or a bad thing.

Preferred negotiating style
The highest score recorded on the Style analysis form (Worksheet 4) indicates your preferred style. If the difference between this and the next highest score is 9 points or more, then it suggests that this preferred style has become 'fixed' and it will be difficult to 'fall back' to another style. If there are two equal highest scores then it suggests that you are ambivalent about these styles. Either could be used with equal facility.

Fall-back style
The second highest score on the Style analysis form is the so-called fall-back style. What this indicates is that when you are under

pressure, you might deviate from your preferred style and slip into the fall-back style. Sometimes this can be a good thing, because the fall-back style might be more effective than the preferred one. (Just think of the number of people who always claim to work better when under pressure!) The converse is true also, thus at times the fall-back style might be less effective.

Statistical 5:5 style

If on the Style analysis form the difference between each score is only a point or so, and the whole range of scores is encompassed by 10–12 points, then it suggests that you have no clearly preferred style. In these circumstances it is termed to be a statistical 5:5 style and should be considered as such, irrespective of what happens to be the highest scoring style on the form.

Style effectiveness

It is generally accepted that the styles discussed rate thus:

9:9   Most effective (a win-win stance, i.e. both salesman and client 'win' – seeking best of all possible worlds).
5:5   Next most effective (half win-half win stance, compromise decisions).
9:1   Effective with inexperienced passive buyers stance (win-lose – can be too forceful for many customers).
1:9   Less effective except perhaps with long standing customers or routine service business (lose-win stance – concessionary).
1:1   Rarely effective (lose-lose stance).

It is quite easy to see how these differences in style effectiveness come about. You could try thinking of as many aspects of negotiations as you can and compare each style against it. If the style will meet that aspect of negotiation it scores one point, if it partly matches it it scores half a point and zero if it fails to match it at all. Some aspects of negotiation are listed below and scored accordingly.

	9:1	1:9	1:1	5:5	9:9
Commitment to task	1	–	–	½	1
Commitment to relationship	–	1	–	½	1
Coping with conflict	½	–	–	½	1
Building on other's ideas	–	1	–	½	1
Prepared to use power	1	–	–	½	1
Flexibility	–	–	–	½	1
Total	2½	2	–	3	6

From these figures it confirms the claim made above that 9:9 is the most effective style and although 5:5 is the next best, it falls very much short of the 9:9. 9:1 is slightly less effective than 5:5 on these scores, but if more factors were considered, 9:1 would be likely to fall even lower in relation to 5:5.

Action plan

From the foregoing analysis of styles and their effectiveness it is clearly desirable for a salesman to develop a negotiating style which approaches 9:9.

According to how you scored yourself in this exercise, there will be two overall strategies open to you to move in the 9:9 direction (assuming that you are not already there).

1 Develop more concern for the customer and his needs. (This will be particularly true for 1:1, 9:1 and to a lesser extent 5:5 scores.)
2 Develop more concern for making the sale. (This will be particularly true for 1:1, 1:9 and to a lesser extent 5:5 scores.)

Only you will be able to ascertain what this will mean in practical terms, but some initial clues will be found by looking back to how you answered the questions in the exercise and identifying where you had low scores.

Chapter 6

Exercise 6.1:   Opportunities to close

In this case study there were several opportunities for Derek James to pick up a buying signal and by doing so, to move the interview in his favour by bringing it nearer to a close.

 Did you spot any of them?

Opportunity 1

Barrett: 'I would really *prefer something a little more rustic.*'

         The nature of this buying signal was Barrett volunteering his personal *preference.* James might have responded something like this:

James: 'I have a few samples of rustic brick in my van. Shall we look at them?'

Opportunity 2

Barrett: 'Oh dear! *I didn't really want to spend too much.* After all, we don't live out in the garden, do we?'

         The nature of the buying signal which is in italics, is an *objection.* James might have responded something like this:

James: 'Yes, I quite understand. (Agreeing.) How much did you imagine spending on the wall then, Mr Barrett?' (Asking a question.)

         With this information in his possession it would be relatively easy for James to come up with a proposition that would fit Mr Barrett's pocket.

Opportunity 3

Barrett: 'Are these bricks *easy to get hold of?*'

Nature of the buying signal, a *question*. James might have responded as follows:

James: 'I'm sure I can get hold of them easily. Is that what you would like me to do, Mr Barrett?'

Opportunity 4

Barrett: 'We would like to get things *moving quickly.*'

Nature of the buying signal, a *committing statement*. James might have responded as follows:

James: 'When exactly would you want the work to start then, Mr Barrett?'

Opportunity 5

Barrett: 'Well, *getting back to the bricks idea*. Can anything be done to stop them absorbing water?'

The nature of this buying signal, which is in italics, is a veiled *committing statement*. Instead of replying as he did, James might have tried:

James: 'Are you beginning to prefer the idea of using bricks then, Mr Barrett?' (Checking it out.)

With this information James could 'tailor' the rest of the interview in the direction favoured by Barrett and thereby improve his chances of reaching a positive conclusion.

Opportunity 6

Barrett: 'Now I'm back where I started. (He sighs.) *I'm really quite confused.*'

The nature of this buying signal is disappointment (body language of a sigh) and the need for more information to dispel the confusion. Again the signal is in italics. Knowing this James could have tried a summary close:

James: 'Well let us try to weigh up the pros and cons of the two types of wall logically. Let's take the brick first Mr Barrett. In it's favour are, (a) it's less expensive, (b) the materials are readily available, (c) your wife likes the idea of brick. The only drawback is the absorption factor, but that can be easily overcome. Now the ornamental bricks – well they certainly look nice but (a) they are more expensive and (b) there could be a delay with the capping. It seems as though brick wins. What do you think Mr Barrett?

Whatever Barrett's reply, James is now much closer to reaching a satisfactory conclusion.

This case study is clearly not a very complex sales situation and yet even then the salesman missed at least six opportunities to move nearer to a close by not spotting the buying signals. Did you spot any other opportunities to close? If there were at least six opportunities to close in this relatively simple situation, just think how many more might arise in a longer or more complex sales interview! Interviews that will be more like the ones that you are likely to have with your prospective clients!

Exercise 6.2:   The quotation

What follows is an example of a 'quotation' which might have been sent to Mr Taylor. It is unlikely that the letter you prepared will be identical to this but it is to be hoped that your thinking as you prepared the quotation embraced the main points listed below.

1 *Nature of the proposal*

Taking into account that the potential client was relatively unsophisticated, the proposal itself was not very complex and the value of the contract not very high, all this points to a simple quotation in the form of a letter. If the reverse had been true i.e. the client was sophisticated, the proposal complex or the value of the contract high, then it might well have merited the quotation being presented as a separate document, with a supporting selling letter.

2 *Layout*

It is largely a matter of personal choice how the final layout will look. Although it isn't essential to have each section numbered and underlined as in the example shown here, all of these topics should have been included somewhere in your letter.

Note:

(a) It is generally recognized as good practice to follow the fee, investment, or whatever (but never the word *cost* if it can be avoided) immediately with the benefits, thereby softening the possible impact of the outlay figure by balancing it with expected savings.

(b) Many people think it is useful to end the letter with a positive phrase or statement. Since the reader often only remembers the ends words, this is seen to be psychologically rewarding for him.

Dear Mr Taylor

I would like to thank you for finding the time for our meeting the other day when you were obviously so busy. You asked me to submit my proposal to you in writing and, taking a leaf out of your book, I've attempted to keep it short and to the point.

1   <u>Your situation</u>
    (a)   You are becoming increasingly busy with new work contracts, many of which require you to employ other people on a sub-contractual basis.
    (b)   Your turnover has increased several fold over the last five years.
    (c)   Your paperwork increases in proportion to the amount of building work you do.
    (d)   All your book-keeping and financial accounts are done by you and your wife, often keeping you both occupied until late into the night.

2   <u>My proposal</u>
    Is that
    (a)   I prepare your annual end of year accounts.
    (b)   I advise you on tax matters.
    (c)   I provide you with financial management advice through-out the year.

3   <u>My background</u>
    I have spent most of my adult life working for nationally known firms of chartered accountants. For the past ten years I have specialized in helping small businesses with their financial management and tax problems. During the last year I have set up my own company specializing in these particular fields of work.

4   <u>Fees</u>
    I estimate that to provide the service my fees will be £650 + VAT + expenses (which will be negligible), payable thus – £300 after 6 months, the remainder at the end of the year.

5   <u>Benefits</u>
    You will benefit from my services in the following ways:

(a) Both you and your wife will have increased leisure time through not having to prepare your own accounts.

(b) Freeing you from some of the non-productive administrative duties will provide you with the opportunity to do more contract work and to earn income.

(c) I have reduced many other clients' tax bills because of my understanding of the tax system. I would anticipate making similar savings for you.

(d) Regular financial management throughout the year will be akin to having a regular check up at the dentist — if any corrective action is required it won't need drastic treatment.

6 Proof

If you wish to check the claims I make, I will be happy to let you speak to some of my clients who run similar businesses to yours. They will be pleased to tell you how I have helped them.

I will phone you next week to hear how you react to this proposal and to see how we might make progress towards what I anticipate will be a very productive collaboration.

Yours sincerely

Dennis Hunt

Exercise 6.3:   Does persistence pay

The narrative clearly raises the question of whether or not persistence pays in selling. Is it a useful asset?

What are the positive points from this story?

- Beryl Reid believed in herself and her sales 'offer'.
- She was never rude.
- She was enthusiastic.
- She was persistent and knew what she wanted.
- She put all her resources into the campaign.
- She made friends in the client system.
- She did in fact have something the buyer wanted.

What are the negative points from this story?

- Was it realistic to expect to be seen without an appointment?
- Was it making the best use of her time?
- Was she too passive?
- She didn't seem to have any alternative strategies to gain an interview.

Lessons for the salesman

Any salesman would be wise to adopt the positive points that emerge from this story. They are all likely to stand him in good stead in any sales interview. Similarly a salesman can also learn from the negative side because he must give consideration to all of these points in his own sales interviews.

Application to a sales situation
1 A salesman must be persistent, but he must channel that persistence into situations that have a real prospect of success – hence the need for careful preparation.
2 Many salesmen give up too easily.
3 Persistence is needed in the sales offer to build agreement stage by stage in order to move to a final close.
4 The best opportunities to close often occur at the first meeting or when something new is being proposed.

Exercise 6.4: *The postmortem*

- Did I make a good impression in the first thirty seconds?
- Was I on time?
- Was I dressed appropriately?
- Did I use a pre-planned opening?
- Was I enthusiastic?
- Did I sell benefits or merely features?
- Was I too glib or insincere?
- Was I insensitive to the buyer's needs?
- Did I make any tactless remarks which upset the buyer?
- Was I properly prepared?
- Did I use 'I' too much and 'you' too little?
- Did I cover all the points I wanted to cover?
- Did I become repetitive?
- Did I ask questions to make trial closes?
- Was I more interested in my sales offer than the client's business?
- Did I listen enough?
- Were my sales aids immaculate?
- Did I use my aids properly?
- Was I overfamiliar/too aloof?
- Was I selling to the right person?
- Did I ask for the order?
- Did I ask why I didn't get the order?

Index

Administrative demands, 49
Advertising and promotion, 27–8
Appointments, 58–61, 86–8
    arrival, 106
    confirming, 70
    handling objections, 67–70
    letter writing, 59
    running late, 73
    speaking to prospect, 64–7
    telephoning, 61–4
    timing, 70–2

Basic research checklist, 29–31
Benefit analysis sheet, 136–7, 145
Benefit selling, 125–8
    communicating benefits, 138–40
    customer appeal, 132–7
    establishing commitment, 134
    identifying benefits, 128–37
    proof, 134
    'so what' test, 134–8
Benefits, 128–31
    company, 130
    differential, 131
    standard, 129
Bribery, 28–9
Buy classes, 5, 16–17
Buy phases, 11–12
Buyers:
    difficult, 24–7, 39
    identifying, 18–19, 23–7
    meeting, 106
    pressure on, 12–15
Buying decisions, 10, 11
Buying signals, 186–9
    body language, 186–7
    committing statements, 187–8
    objections, 187

Closing the sale, 66–7, 184–203
    alternative closes, 189–99
    asking for the order, 189, 195
    buying signals, 186–9
    concession closes, 195–6
    forcing questions, 191–3
    opportunities, 185–6
    pitfalls, 199–201
    post mortem on no sales, 202
    quotation closes, 196–9
    summary closes, 193–5
    trial closes, 190–1
Communication skills, 138–40
Complaints, 48
Complexity of service, 10
Confidence, 109–14
Consultant role, 21
Cost of service, 10–11
Credit-worthiness, 167–8
Customer analysis form, 41
Customer appeal, 132–7
Customers:
    analysis, 38–9
    appointments, 58–61, 86–8
    call rates, 52
    call strategies, 82
    classifying, 51
    pinpointing, 51–2
    ranking, 77–8
    reaching, 47–8
    research checklist, 29–31
see also Buyers

Decision-making-unit (D.M.U.), 10,
    11, 12, 15, 16, 17, 18
Demonstrations, 98–9, 104
Discounts, 150, 167
Drinking habits, 107

Entertaining, 28
Ethical considerations, 27–9

Individuals, selling to, 15–16
Information officer role, 20
Interviews, obtaining, 57–8

Jargon, 146–8
Job satisfaction, 34–7

Letters, initial, 83–6
Liability to customer, 29
Listening, 115–18

Monitoring, 12
Motivation, 37

Negotiator role, 22–3, 177–83
Newness of service, 10

Objections:
    to appointments, 67–70
    as buying signal, 187
    delay, 160–2
    feature, 156–9
    fundamental, 151–2, 153–5
    handling, 149–68
    hidden, 162–3
    information seeking, 68–9, 159
    loyalty, 163–5
    price, 165–7
    standard, 152, 155–6
Objections analysis sheet, 157
Opening interview, 64–5, 90
    action planning, 92–101
    call objectives, 90–1
    choice of venue, 99–100
    meeting the buyer, 106
    opening statement, 100–1, 114
    pre-call planning, 90
    spoilers, 107–8
    successful openings, 101–6
    supporting material and visual aids,
        96–9

Organization, selling to, 9–10

Problem definition, 11
Problem identification, 11
Product element of service, 7–8

Quotations, 196–9, 207–9

References, 102–3

Sales aids, 103–4
Sales letters, 83–6
Sales strategy, 19–20
Sales territory:
    dividing, 53
    mapping, 51
    minimizing travel, 53–6
    organizing, 53
    planning, 50–3
Salesman:
    areas of work, 19–20
    breakdown of daily activity, 49–50
    motivation, 37
    personal appearance, 107
    roles, 20–3
Secretaries, dealing with, 63–4
Selling a service v. a product, 6–9
Senior executives, meeting, 19
'So what' test, 134–8
Solution specification, 12
Spoilers, 107–8
Style analysis form, 182
Switchboard operators, dealing with,
    63

Telephoning, 61–4
Territory planning, 50–7, 76–81
Travel minimizing, 53–6
Trust, element of, 7

Venue, choice of, 99–100
Visual aids, 96–9

Workload, 52